Presenting
M. E. Kerr

Twayne's
Young Adult
Authors Series

General Editor: Ron Brown, Boston Public Library

This series seeks to meet the need for critical
studies of fiction for young adults. Each
volume examines the life and work of one
author, helping both teachers and readers of
young adult literature to understand better
the writers they have read with such pleasure
and fascination.

Presenting
M. E. Kerr

Alleen Pace Nilsen

Illustrated by Meg Kelleher

Twayne Publishers
A Division of G.K. Hall & Co. • Boston

To
Don L. F. Nilsen,
my good humor man

Presenting M. E. Kerr

Alleen Pace Nilsen

Copyright © 1986 by G. K. Hall & Co.
All Rights Reserved
Published by Twayne Publishers
A Division of G. K. Hall & Co.
70 Lincoln Street, Boston, Massachusetts 02111

Copyediting supervised by Lewis DeSimone
Book design and production by Marne B. Sultz

Typeset in Century Schoolbook by
Compset, Inc. of Beverly, Massachusetts

Printed on permanent/durable acid-free
paper and bound in the United States of America

Library of Congress Cataloging in Publication Data

Nilsen, Alleen Pace.
Presenting M. E. Kerr.

(Twayne's young adult authors series)
Bibliography: p. 134
Includes index.
1. Kerr, M. E.—Criticism and interpretation.
2. Young adult fiction, American—History and criticism.
I. Title   II. Title: M. E. Kerr.   III. Series: Twayne's
young adult authors.
PS3561.E643Z786   1986   813'.54   86-4297
ISBN 0-8057-8202-8

Contents

Preface

Anyone listing today's best writers for young adults would have to place M. E. Kerr very near the top not only for her writing ability but also for her consistency in producing a dozen highly acclaimed and popular books between 1972 and 1985. There are four main reasons that I enjoyed rereading these twelve books in preparation for writing this critique. First, M. E. Kerr is entertaining. She believes in the maxim that one of the editors of *Punch* used to preach to his contributors: Even when you can't be funny, be interesting. Second, because she centers her stories around a contemporary problem or issue, she leaves readers with something to ponder after their smiles have faded. Instead of providing pat answers, she brings up the kinds of questions that lead to thinking and insights. Third, she exudes intellectual curiosity and an enthusiasm for intriguing facts. She gives her readers healthy chunks of information packaged in relevant contexts rather than in the randomness of a game of Trivial Pursuit. And fourth, M. E. Kerr is a good writer. Her style is unique in young adult literature and no other YA author approaches language with the same skill.

My hope is that reading this volume will not take the place of reading M. E. Kerr's books, but instead will encourage adults as well as teenagers to read her stories with more insight and pleasure.

I am grateful to M. E. Kerr (Marijane Meaker) for being generous with her time and thoughts when I interviewed her on 28 May 1985. Statements from Kerr made throughout this book and not attributed to other sources come from this interview. I am also

Preface

grateful to Ron Brown for inviting me to embark on the project, to Ken Donelson for sharing his thoughts and those of his students, to Caroline Birdsall and Athenaide Dallett for editorial help and advice, and to William Morris of Harper & Row, who over the years has supplied me with review copies of Kerr's books. Finally, I am indebted to Gale Research's *Something About the Author Autobiography Series,* Volume One (1986) for much of the biographical information in Chapter 1.

Alleen Pace Nilsen

Tempe, Arizona

Chronology

1927 Marijane Meaker born 27 May in Auburn, New York.

1943 Leaves Auburn to attend Stuart Hall school in Staunton, Virginia.

1945 Is suspended from Stuart Hall in February, but allowed to return in April and graduate with her class. Attends Vermont Junior College, where she edits the school newspaper.

1946 Enrolls at the University of Missouri.

1949 Graduates from the University of Missouri as an English literature major, moves to New York to find a job in publishing.

1951 Sells "Devotedly, Patrick Henry Casebolt" (under pen name Laura Winston) to *Ladies' Home Journal*.

1952 *Spring Fire* and *Dark Intruder* (under pen name Vin Packer).

1953 *Look Back to Love* (under pen name Vin Packer).

1954 *Come Destroy Me* and *Whisper His Sin* (under pen name Vin Packer).

1955 *We Walk Alone* (under pen name Ann Aldrich). *The Thrill Kids* (under pen name Vin Packer).

1956 *Dark Don't Catch Me* and *The Young and Violent* (under pen name Vin Packer).

1957 *Three-Day Terror* (under pen name Vin Packer).

1958 *We Too Must Love* (under pen name Ann Aldrich). *The Evil Friendship* and *5:45 to Suburbia* (under pen name Vin Packer).

Chronology

1959 *The Twisted Ones* (under pen name Vin Packer).

1960 *Carol in a Thousand Cities* (under pen name Ann Aldrich).

1961 *The Girl on the Best Seller List* and *Something in the Shadows* (under pen name Vin Packer).

1962 *Intimate Victims* (under pen name Vin Packer).

1963 *We Two Won't Last* (under pen name Ann Aldrich). *Alone at Night* (under pen name Vin Packer).

1964 *Sudden Endings* (under M. J. Meaker; paperback edition under pen name Vin Packer).

1967 *Hometown* (under M. J. Meaker). *The Hare in March* (under pen name Vin Packer).

1968 *Game of Survival* (under Marijane Meaker).

1969 *Don't Rely on Gemini* (under pen name Vin Packer).

1972 *Shockproof Sydney Skate* (under Marijane Meaker). *Take a Lesbian to Lunch* (under pen name Ann Aldrich). *Dinky Hocker Shoots Smack!* (under pen name M. E. Kerr).

1973 *If I Love You, Am I Trapped Forever?* (under pen name M. E. Kerr).

1974 *The Son of Someone Famous* (under pen name M. E. Kerr).

1975 *Is That You, Miss Blue?* and *Love Is a Missing Person* (under pen name M. E. Kerr).

1977 *I'll Love You When You're More Like Me* (under pen name M. E. Kerr).

1978 *Gentlehands* (under pen name M. E. Kerr).

1981 *Little Little* (under pen name M. E. Kerr).

1982 *What I Really Think of You* (under pen name M. E. Kerr).

1983 *ME ME ME ME ME* (under pen name M. E. Kerr).

1984 *Him She Loves?* (under pen name M. E. Kerr).

1985 *I Stay Near You* (under pen name M. E. Kerr).

Dinky Hocker Shoots Smack!

1. The Person

Although there is no definitive description of the typical writer for young adults, it is safe to say that if and when someone devises such a statement it will not be a close description of M. E. Kerr. She never taught high school as did such popular writers as Robin Brancato, Paula Danziger, Richard Peck, and Paul Zindel. She does not have teenage children of her own to inspire her or act as critics as do Judy Blume, Sue Ellen Bridgers, Robert Cormier, Lois Duncan, Norma and Harry Mazer, and Norma Klein. And unlike Maureen Daly, who wrote *Seventeenth Summer* while she was a college student, and S. E. Hinton, who wrote *The Outsiders* while she was a teenager, Kerr writes from memories that are three or four decades old. She was in her mid-forties when she wrote her first YA novel, *Dinky Hocker Shoots Smack!*

Few other writers for teenagers came to the field with an equivalent background of experience. Kerr had already published five books under the pseudonym Ann Aldrich, twenty primarily suspense novels under the name Vin Packer, three novels under her actual name of Marijane Meaker, and one nonfiction book about suicide under her initials, M. J. Meaker. She had also published a few short stories under her "happy pen name," Laura Winston, and numerous made-to-order confession stories under various made-to-order names.

When Norma Fox Mazer did a 1985 survey of fellow writers of young adult books, Kerr again stood out from the crowd because of her working methods. She is the only one in the group (Robin Brancato, Judy Blume, Sue Ellen Bridgers, Lois Duncan, Norma Klein, Robert Lipsyte, Marilyn Sachs, and Hilma Wolitzer) who does not discuss her work in its early stages or give her manuscripts to someone for reading before mailing them to her editors. Kerr said that she works as a loner, keeping each book in its own little world, because she is too paranoid for sample opinions. Paradoxically, her courage impressed Mazer, who said, "To write one's book without ever asking for confirmation from some trusted other struck me as an act of bravery similar to plunging into an icy northern lake in January and swimming from one shore to the other with no one in sight."[1]

Getting to know M. E. Kerr the person is both easier and more difficult than getting to know other authors for young adults. It is more difficult because Kerr is somewhat of a loner, staying home and writing rather than going out on speaking tours. As she once explained to a radio interviewer, she does not like to travel, and meeting her readers usually requires a trip. In the late 1970s when she attended her first American Library Association convention, she was happily surprised to discover that talking with people who had read her books was actually fun, but getting there was still a chore.

Although she makes five or six presentations a year, she turns down more speaking engagements than she accepts, and she does not go out of her way to be interviewed, which works against her developing an easy familiarity with those teachers and librarians who are the ones most likely to introduce her books to young readers. Also, the fact that she has written under so many pseudonyms makes it harder for readers and critics to look at her work as a continuous whole. On the other hand, Kerr includes so much of herself in her books that careful readers can come away feeling well acquainted with a very interesting person.

Getting to Know M. E. Kerr through *ME ME ME ME ME*

To become acquainted with M. E. Kerr, the best place to start is her autobiographical collection of eleven short stories entitled *ME ME ME ME ME: Not a Novel,* published in 1983. Kerr, who was born in Auburn, New York, in 1927 as the middle child and only daughter of Ellis R. and Ida T. Meaker, presents these stories in more or less chronological order going from her World War II childhood to her beginning career days as a free-lance New York writer in the 1950s.

"'Murder' He Says" was probably chosen as the opening story because it is the most romantic and was therefore judged the most likely to interest teenage readers. It is the story of fifteen-year-old Marijane's "romance" with Donald Dare, the son of the local undertaker. (He later served as the prototype for the fictional Wally Witherspoon in *I'll Love You When You're More Like Me*.) Marijane and Donald's romance, however, isn't nearly as interesting as the one between her best friend, Ella Gwen Logan, and Hyman Ginzburg. Hyman, a Jewish refugee from Nazi Germany, moves to Auburn when he is almost eighteen. Besides speaking three languages, he wears old-fashioned gold-rimmed glasses, collects stamps, and plays both the violin and the piano. There were very few Jews in Auburn, and the word *hyman* "was never spoken unless you were talking privately about the wedding night." Hyman, who is 6'4" tall, "made everything all the worse for himself by refusing all invitations to go out for basketball." The other students call him "Hyman the Hopeless" or just plain "Hopeless." He was the real life inspiration for the fictional Doomed in *If I Love You, Am I Trapped Forever?*

Marijane, Hyman, and Ella Gwen are the three library freaks in town. One ordinary winter afternoon when Marijane has just discovered Thomas Wolfe and is rushing to find Ella Gwen and show her a sexy passage about "black, bitter, aching loneliness," she sees Hyman and Ella Gwen kissing, right there in the stacks between Louisa May Alcott and James Joyce. It is a long, long kiss that in a few short seconds outdistances Marijane: "They were wired for sound, and I was not even plugged in." What Marijane happens to witness is the beginning of a "love affair that Shakespeare, MGM, or Cole Porter couldn't have made more passionate and doomed."

When Hyman is drafted and told to report to Fort Knox, Kentucky, Marijane and Donald help Ella Gwen run away with him. It is after this momentous event—what Marijane later characterized as "her finest hour"—that the Meakers decide it is time for Marijane to go away to boarding school. They look at the advertisements in the back pages of *Good Housekeeping* magazine and select Stuart Hall near Staunton, Virginia—but before sharing that adventure with readers Kerr goes back to present three stories from her childhood.

Prior to World War II, Marijane's father was a mayonnaise manufacturer. During the war, however, mayonnaise isn't considered essential, and so Mr. Meaker has to switch over to dehydrating onions. The whole town smells like onions, and it is little comfort to Marijane that her father places apologetic ads in the local newspaper:

> Ivanhoe Foods Has Gone to War!
> Our onions are for field rations for our fighting men.
> When you smell onions, pray for peace.

Marijane's father provides her with alternate moments of pride and chagrin. In World War I, he served in the French army and he nostalgically wears a French beret when he rides his bicycle back and forth to work. He is slightly deaf and uses a hearing aid in one ear. Every Sunday morning in church he ceremoniously takes it out and puts it away as the minister begins his sermon. He is just as obvious in replacing it before the choir begins singing.

Ellis Meaker is bookish, reading everything from the Harvard Classics to all the Book of the Month Club selections and in between Dickens, Emerson, Poe, Steinbeck, and such magazines as *Time, Life, Look,* and *Fortune.* It is from his example that Marijane develops the habit of reading. The family living room is four walls of books, and Mr. Meaker seems constantly to be investigating some person or some period of history. Marijane spends hours browsing in the town library while waiting for her father to do his research. He keeps a daily journal and encourages Marijane to keep a diary. "Men keep journals, and women keep diaries," he explains. He is more faithful about his journal than Marijane is about her diary. In an author's note, Kerr says that without his journal, she couldn't have remembered things nearly as well.

The second story in *ME ME ME ME ME* is "Where Are You Now, William Shakespeare?" Of this period in Kerr's life, Ellis Meaker writes "Marijane is ten. She plays with boys and looks like one." She dresses in her brother's outgrown pants and old shirts, set off by one of her father's business suit vests, a cap, and Indian moccasins. She has a ten-year-old boyfriend named William Shakespeare, called Billy for short. Unlike Donald Dare, Kerr writes, he does not "call at seven for dates, or suffer my father's inspection, or give me a silver identification bracelet." They do not have a song, either. Mostly they catch sunfish and polliwogs at Hoopes Park and talk about the future. Billy Shakespeare accepts the fact that Marijane's real hero is her father, and they both agree that if they ever marry and have a son they will name him Ellis rather than William. Billy insists that this isn't because William Shakespeare is a funny name; "It's just that there's a famous writer with the same name."

Marijane is sure that if only her father were president the country wouldn't be having so many troubles. Billy not-so-tactfully points out that Mr. Meaker would have to be elected first. Marijane is convinced that this would be no problem, and after consulting her father explains to Billy that the only thing standing in the way is Mr. Meaker's desire for privacy for himself and his family.

The third story is "Marijane the Spy," the most powerful in the book, discussed here in chapter 2. The fourth one has the strange title of "1, 2, 3, 4, 5, 6, 7, 8, 9, 10, 11, 12, 100." The explanation comes early in the story: "Twelve was the age I was when my baby brother was born, and my older brother went off to military school. Thirteen was the year I became a hundred." Marijane feels like a "nothing, sandwiched between two stars." To get her out of her "slump," Mrs. Meaker enrolls Marijane in Laura Bryan's school for ballroom dancing. Here Marijane is trapped in a Catch-22 situation. Mrs. Meaker, who is eager that Marijane become a social success, keeps wondering aloud why no boy invites Marijane to stay afterwards and go to Miss Margaret's ice cream parlor for a soda. At least Clinton Klock, a boy still in his formative years and not yet "up to snuff," dances with Marijane every week between 4:00 and 5:00, but he never mentions a soda. Finally, after weeks of Mrs. Meaker's inquisitions and Marijane's weak excuses, Marijane takes matters into her own hands and asks Clinton why they never go for a soda. When he says he is saving his money to buy a boat, Marijane offers to go dutch. When he is still hesitant, Marijane offers to treat.

She thinks she is going to be saved from "Life's Biggest Embarrassment" by the fact that no one will know she is treating since she has slipped Clinton the money. But after this grand social experience, during which Marijane unfairly signals to her friends that she knows this boy is a loser and that she has come with him only for laughs, Clinton and Marijane go out to find Mrs. Klock waiting in the car to give them a ride. Marijane thinks little of this until she arrives home and is met by her indignant and embarrassed mother: "Whatever got into you to tell Clinton you'd buy him a soda! When he called his mother to tell her why he'd be late getting home, she felt so ashamed, she got dressed and got out the car, to give you a ride home! She said Clinton has money of his own, but he's saving for a boat, and she felt just awful!"

Marijane feels like throwing up, especially when her mother goes on to preach that obviously Marijane has too much money to squander, and if she feels so rich why doesn't she think of buying a present for her baby brother?

The fifth story, "There's Not a Man in This Damn Nunnery," recounts Marijane's experience of going away to Stuart Hall. First semester she is assigned to live with Kay Walters, the first P.K. (preacher's kid) that Marijane has known. Second semester she is moved next door to the deaf Agnes Thatcher, the first handicapped person she has known. Parts of this story are drawn almost word-for-word from *Is That You, Miss Blue?*, but an interesting difference is how much more candid Kerr is in this autobiographical story about the lesbian kissing games that the girls play. In an afterword, Kerr explains that "Like all true experiences that are later translated into fiction, some of it was that way, some of it wasn't that way, and sometimes the author no longer remembers what was and what wasn't."

"Your Daddy Was a Sailor" is the heading of chapter 6, taken from the title of one of the sad, romantic stories that Kerr began writing and submitting to magazines between her junior and senior years. She is especially fond of this title because an editor wrote "Touching" on a rejection slip, which Marijane carried for weeks in the back pocket of her jeans.

In 1944, the town of Auburn is full of sailors from Sampson Naval Base, and that is one of the reasons the Meaker family buys a summer cottage out at the furthest point on Owasco Lake. During that period, Marijane becomes Eric Ranthram McKay.

By day I swam and sailed and looked after my kid brother, listening to my girl friends' accounts of what was happening, for hours on the telephone. By night I wrote, using my first pseudonym . . . chosen because my father's initials were E. R. M. After I wrote a story, I mailed it off to a magazine with a letter written on my father's stationery, engraved with his initials and our home address.

A highlight of the summer is a visit from Jan Fox, supposedly the most sophisticated girl at Stuart Hall. Marijane, who no longer believes that her father would be president of the United States if only he did not value the family's privacy, is terribly humiliated when her father makes their dates come in and show their drivers' licenses. In a wonderful Kerr line, Marijane laments "I wished I was Eric Ranthram McKay, back upstairs where I belonged, writing about life instead of enduring it."

In an insightful afterword, Kerr explains that she was probably drawn to a pen name not only because of her father's monogrammed stationery, but also because she liked the idea that she could create a separate identity for herself and write about people she knew without them ever knowing who was telling their secrets.

"What I Did between Trains," the seventh story, tells how Marijane is expelled—or suspended (there's some disagreement about the matter)—from Stuart Hall because on her way back to school after Christmas vacation she buys a dart board that she decorates with yearbook pictures of faculty members accompanied by disrespectful names. This popular dormitory game is found in Marijane's closet by the house mother, and on George Couldn't-Tell-A-Lie Washington's birthday, she is sent home.

Marijane's family is more understanding and supportive than she dreamed they would be. In fact, her mother is primarily relieved. The suspension came four days prior to the opening of the school play, *The Importance of Being Earnest* by Oscar Wilde. For months, Marijane has been practicing the part of Algernon Moncrieff. Mrs. Meaker does not want her daughter dressing in nineteenth-century drag, no matter how literary the purpose.

From the end of February through March, Marijane works in a local defense plant while her mother and father write letters to get her back in school. In April, she is back, but because the school yearbook was put together while she was gone, all they could do was stick her at the end of the alphabet, ". . . Wellford, Worthy and Yates . . . then Marijane Meaker, on record forever, the out-of-line black sheep."

Chapter 8, "The Sister of Someone Famous," is about Marijane's first college experience. She had wanted to go to the University of Missouri School of Journalism because it was considered the best in the country. Her father argues that she should go to Syracuse University so she will marry a New York boy and the Meakers can know their grandchildren. The argument over Syracuse University and the University of Missouri becomes a moot question because Marijane's records and recommendations from Stuart Hall are so bad that she isn't accepted by either place. However, Vermont Junior College decides to take a chance on her. There, a wise teacher makes her founding editor of a school newspaper. Her first published story is in this paper—never mind that she is the editor and practically the whole staff.

A story within this story is about one of the students whose sister is a famous movie star. Marijane's crowd is skeptical and in fact downright mean about what they judge to be a false claim to glory. When they are finally proven wrong, the little sister is extremely gracious about the matter. This experience made Kerr begin thinking about the pressures on those who live close to celebrities and eventually resulted in her book *The Son of Someone Famous.*

After Marijane's first year, when she does surprisingly well at the junior college, she is accepted at the University of Missouri School of Journalism for the fall of 1946. However, she hadn't anticipated one problem: in this era of postwar growth and housing shortages, there is no place for out-of-state students to live. She will have to get into a sorority or return home. Her father does little to boost her confidence when he refuses to ship her trunk until after the horrendous event that Kerr describes in chapter 9, "Rush Week." Even though Marijane hates much of what occurs that week, she is relieved to be invited to join Alpha Delta Pi. It is from her experiences with sororities that Kerr created the title of her sixth YA book, *I'll Love You When You're More Like Me.* It seems to Marijane that sororities say to their members: don't be individuals; be as much like the group as possible.

Kerr pursues this theme further in chapter 10, "Sorority Life," where as might be expected Marijane is not the typical sister. She feels drawn to other journalism students, most of whom are independents, and to campus intellectuals as much as she does to her housemates. The journalism students encourage each other in their writing. They have a saying that "You'd never commit suicide as long as you had a manuscript in the mail. The trick was to keep your stories circulating; always have at least one 'out.'" About this time, Marijane becomes interested in F. Scott Fitzgerald and wears out a copy of his autobiographical pieces called *The Crack-Up.* She circles words like *insouciance* and memorizes his line about good writing being swimming underwater and holding your breath. At a sorority masquerade party she goes as a rejection slip, wearing a full-length black slip with rejections from magazines pinned to it.

The summer of 1948, Marijane falls in love with a Hungarian refugee who is a revolutionary of sorts, joins the Communist party, and starts working as a volunteer at the Fulton mental hospital. When her revolutionary grows too busy for her and does

things that disillusion her, she begins dating the head psychiatrist at the mental hospital. She also dates an English major and
switches her program from journalism to English literature because she decides she does not want to be restricted to facts. She
wants the freedom of adding her own ideas and conjectures. Else-
where, she confesses that the decision to change was also influenced by the fact that she failed economics, which was a basic
requirement for journalism majors.

The concluding chapter of Kerr's *ME ME ME ME ME* is entitled "New York" and tells how after graduation Marijane moves
with two other Missouri graduates to New York City, where she
manages to get hired and fired by nine different companies in a
single year. Then on 20 April 1951, when she is twenty-three
years old, she makes her first big sale. *Ladies Home Journal* buys
her short story "Devotedly, Patrick Henry Casebolt" for $750 and
Kerr never works at a full-time job again.

Getting to Know Kerr through
Her Other Writings and Interviews

ME ME ME ME ME is not the only book in which M. E. Kerr—
the person—appears; it is just the most obvious. In reality, her
personality is the driving force behind many of her most interesting characters. She explains in an autobiographical piece that by
the time she was in her forties she was no longer very interested
in murder and crime. She became more mellow and began seeing
"the light *and* the dark. . . . As I looked back on my life, things
seemed funnier to me than they used to. *I* seemed funnier to me
than I used to, and so did a lot of what I'd suffered.'"

After this realization, Kerr sat down to make notes for future
stories. Things that had happened long ago came back to her clear
as a bell, "still ringing": "and making me smile and shake my
head as I realized I had stories in me about *me*—no longer dis-
guised as a homicidal maniac, or a twisted criminal bent on a
scam, but as the smalltown kid I'd been, so typically American

and middleclass and yes, vulnerable, but not as tragic and complicated as I used to imagine."[2]

More than most writers, Kerr interweaves her real life, both past and present, into her writing. The setting for many of her stories is Cayuta, New York, which is a slightly fictionalized version of her old hometown of Auburn, located in Cayuga County. Other books are set in Seaview, based on East Hampton, Long Island, where she now lives.

Names of people she has known and been fascinated by are sprinkled through her books like good luck charms. Sidney is a favorite name for boys, Belle a favorite for girls, and Blessing and Pennington favorites for families. In *I'll Love You When You're More Like Me,* Kerr names her teenage soap opera star, Sabra St. Amour, after an Auburn high school French teacher. In many of her books she names a minor character after Ernest Leogrande, a man she met on the train when she was first traveling to college in Missouri. He was a writer who moved to New York about the same time she did. He wrote for the *New York Daily,* and until his death in 1985 was Kerr's friend and confidante. She started putting his name in her Vin Packer books and kept the custom going for fun.

In the autobiographical piece she did for Gale Research Company, she gives her father credit for making her into a reader while she gives her mother credit for making her into a people watcher and consequently a writer. Long before J. D. Salinger had one of his characters peek into someone else's bathroom cabinet to examine the prescription medicine being used in the household, Mrs. Meaker made this a regular part of her visiting ritual.

On Saturday evenings she would take out her Chevrolet coupe and she and Marijane would drive downtown and park at key vantage points. Mrs. Meaker would knit while she kept up a continuous stream of observations about who was going to the Auburn Palace theater with whom, which men were spending Saturday night at Boysen's Bar, and then on the way home whose house still needed painting, who was eating dinner in their dining room instead of their kitchen, and whose car was parked in whose driveway. In *The Son of Someone Famous* this scene is played out almost word-for-word with Brenda Belle Blossom and her mother.

Another real-life scene that finds its way into Kerr's books is Mrs. Meaker's telephone calls to her friends. She would tell Marijane to go outside and play. Marijane would pretend to obey, slamming the back door on her way to hiding in the hall. Kerr says that eavesdropping on these phone conversations is what taught her how fiction spins grandly from fact. Every conversation started with "Wait 'till you hear this!" Today when Kerr thinks about story ideas, she asks herself if whatever she has thought of could be one of her mother's wait-'till-you-hear-this telephone calls. If the answer is no, then she passes up that idea for a better one.

In nearly every one of Kerr's books, she includes some reference to differences in life-styles and values related to socioeconomic levels or ethnic identification. Kerr's mother sensitized her to such differences.

Ida Meaker "married up," a fact that Kerr says her mother was proud of in her hometown of Syracuse but defensive about in Auburn. Because Ellis Meaker was a local businessman, Mrs. Meaker was especially concerned that the family not offend the townspeople of Auburn. She would cut the labels from coats and sweaters purchased at the big stores in Syracuse lest someone at Second Presbyterian church would notice the lack of support for the hometown merchants. Then she would sew the labels back in prior to visiting her Syracuse relatives. This self-consciousness about labels is one of the details that Kerr uses in *Gentlehands* to illustrate the contrasting social levels of Skye Pennington and Buddy Boyle.

There were very few Jews in Auburn when the Schwartzes, a childless couple, moved into the Meaker neighborhood. Marijane was surprised at the ripple of adult prejudice that their coming set off. In spite of this, or perhaps because of it, Marijane made friends, and their house became her second home. Mrs. Meaker, forever anxious not to offend, instructed Marijane that instead of referring to the Schwartzes as Jewish, she should say that they were "of the Jewish persuasion." In *If I Love You, Am I Trapped*

Forever?, Kerr makes use of this quaint phraseology to illustrate Alan Bennet's naïveté.

Mrs. Meaker was too sensitive to describe anyone as "rich." She would either whisper or spell the word, much as Mildred does in *I Stay Near You.* Mrs. Meaker also taught Marijane such gems of folk wisdom as the following, all of which have found their way into Kerr's books:

> If you marry a Catholic, there'll be one baby right after the other.
>
> If you marry a boy whose father is bald, he will be bald himself one day.
>
> If you marry an Italian, you won't be allowed to wash the salad bowl; they just wipe them out.
>
> If you marry a mortician, you'll have to do the cosmetic work on the corpses because undertaking is a family business.

Kerr treats these not as facts to be learned but as amusing examples of stereotypes that she expects her readers to think about and question.

She accomplishes something similar through having her characters make statements that sound so much like the ideas and philosophies that Kerr has expressed in interviews and essays that one suspects it is really Kerr who, as Adam Blessing's father in *The Son of Someone Famous,* advises his son, "Never discuss manifest knowledge. If you can't be original, be silent." Kerr's wittiness shines through Wally's little sister, who in *I'll Love You When You're More Like Me,* explains that "The dead are no different from you or me, they're just in another stage of development." Kerr's cynicism makes Dinky Hocker complain that "The meek inherit the shaft," and makes Carolyn Cardmaker in *Is That You, Miss Blue?* form an atheists' club to protest the hypocrisy that condemns her minister father to work in poverty-stricken parishes because he criticizes certain church practices.

Kerr's sense of realism comes through when the gay Charlie Gilhooley in *I'll Love You When You're More Like Me* bitterly explains, "You can make straight *A*'s and *A* + 's for ten years of school, and on one afternoon, in a weak moment, confess you think you're gay. What do you think you'll be remembered as thereafter? Not the straight *A* student." In *If I Love You, Am I Trapped Forever?* Kerr's romanticism makes Sophie ask why everyone should take a lot of dull reality seriously when they've got an interesting act like Doomed and Gwendolyn Graney to watch. In *What I Really Think of You,* Kerr's active mind makes her sympathize with Seal von Hennig, who loses her P.K. (preacher's kid) boyfriend when she interrupts a long, passionate kiss to tell him about a new idea she has for telephone tithing. Likewise, Kerr understands the teacher part of Brenda Belle Blossom, who in *The Son of Someone Famous* takes her boyfriend a sweet potato plant and explains:

> "Since we're going steady now, I'm teaching you about beautiful things . . . since I'm not a beautiful thing."
> "I don't get you, Brenda Belle."
> "This will become a beautiful thing, but after it's a beautiful thing for a while, it'll change," I said.
> "How will it change?"
> "It'll begin to stink," I said. "It will make you realize that beauty is not that big a deal, just in case you wish you were going steady with a beauty contest winner."

Kerr's Career

People have talked about how remarkable it is that Kerr found a new kind of writing, a new audience, so late in life. In fact, it isn't Kerr who changed so much as it is her market. She took a twenty-year round trip through the world of a professional writer and then came back to where she started.

Her first breakthrough as an author was the story she sold in 1951 to *Ladies' Home Journal.* At the time, this was a top market for American fiction writers. Among the contributors in the 1950 and 1951 issues were such notables as Shirley Jackson, Rumer

Godden, Jessamyn West, John P. Marquand, and Daphne du Maurier. Kerr was thrilled at selling the story—even when she misread the acceptance letter and thought she was getting $75 instead of $750.

The story, "Devotedly, Patrick Casebolt," published in September 1951, is strictly a young adult romance. Although published under the pen name of Laura Winston, it is immediately recognizable because it is so typically Kerr. It is set in a boarding school much like the one that Flanders Brown goes to in *Is That You, Miss Blue?* The opening is just as offbeat and intriguing as are the leads in Kerr's young adult novels. "A Paul Jones is a deviation of the old game of musical chairs, only instead of sitting on what you are in front of when the music stops, you dance with it. That was how I first met Patrick Henry Casebolt." Most of the story is told through the funny letters that the narrator and Patrick Henry Casebolt send back and forth.

Today some sharp editor might have noticed Kerr's ear for dialogue and her deft touch at comedy and invited her to try her hand at a novel for young adults. This happened to Paul Zindel in the mid 1960s when Charlotte Zolotow, children's book editor at Harper and Row, saw a television production of Zindel's Pulitzer prize-winning play *The Effect of Gamma Rays on Man-in-the-Moon Marigolds* and invited him to write a book for teenagers. The result of this invitation was the ground-breaking and highly acclaimed *The Pigman,* published in 1968. But in 1951, publishers were not thinking of producing books specifically for teenagers.

Kerr did sell a few teen stories to *Compact,* a short-lived magazine for young people. And Bruce Gould, the editor of *Ladies' Home Journal,* liked "Devotedly, Patrick Casebolt" so much that he came to New York to talk with Marijane Meaker, whom he thought was Laura Winston's agent, to see if Winston would be interested in moving to Philadelphia and working with a new column that the magazine wanted to start for young people. The history of young adult literature might have been different if Kerr had accepted, but she declined mainly because she did not want to leave New York City. However, during the conversation, she confessed that she was both Marijane Meaker, the literary agent, and Laura Winston, the twenty-three-year-old author of the story.

Gould thought Kerr's double role was so interesting that he decided to use it in a publicity campaign for the *Ladies' Home Journal*. He arranged for Kerr to be interviewed on several radio shows, one of them conducted by the well-known Mary Margaret McBride. Dick Carroll, an editor at Fawcett Publications, was listening and heard Kerr say that one of the menial jobs she had held the year before had been as a reader at Fawcett. He contacted her and asked if she would be interested in writing a book set in a boarding school for a new line of original paperbacks to be called Gold Medal Books. Kerr countered with the suggestion of a book set in a sorority house since she was much closer to that, and in fact was still living with three sorority sisters transplanted from the University of Missouri to New York City.

Carroll asked for a few chapters and an outline, which Kerr submitted within a few months. Carroll called her for lunch, and as they taxied to the restaurant, she remembers going "under the ramp near Grand Central Station, and in that dark tunnel he told me, 'We're taking your story. I'm advancing you $2,000.'" When the taxi emerged into the sunlight of Park Avenue, Kerr was under contract for her first novel. She wrote the book and named it *Sorority Girl,* but her editor preferred the title *Spring Fire,* adapted from *The Fires of Spring,* a currently popular novel by James Michener.

Kerr explained that for its time, the book was rather sensational, dealing with lesbianism in a sorority. It was an instant paperback success selling over one million copies in 1952. It has long been out of print, but it established Kerr as a novelist and provided her with enough money to take a trip to Europe and move to an apartment without roommates. She moved to a small building (ten apartments in all) on East 94th Street, where she lived for eight years.

One of her neighbors was Tom Baird, an art historian who worked at the Frick Museum. They became close friends and he too began writing. Kerr thinks that one day he looked over her shoulder as she was typing and said to himself "*I* can do that."

She was still playing literary agent, partly because it was fun and partly because it made it so much easier to say nice things about her own work. She sold Baird's first short story for him, the only piece she ever sold for a legitimate client. He began by writing for adults, but now has two young adult novels, including *Walk Out a Brother.*

Kerr lived in New York City from 1949 until 1973, a period she describes as the best of times. Her working relationship with Fawcett must have been mutually satisfactory because she worked with the company for almost ten years, writing mostly suspense stories under the names Vin Packer and Ann Aldrich. She chose that genre because mysteries were the only original paperbacks that had a chance of getting reviewed. Anthony Boucher, columnist for the *New York Times,* gave Kerr enough positive encouragement that she wrote twenty Vin Packer novels before she grew tired and went on to other things.

In 1964 Kerr turned from fictional homicide to real-life suicide and wrote a hardcover book for Doubleday entitled *Sudden Endings.* Also published as a Vin Packer paperback, it consists of case studies of the deaths of famous people including Virginia Woolf, Ernest Hemingway, Hart Crane, Marilyn Monroe, and Joseph Goebbels. Kerr was disappointed that her editor would not let her make conjectures beyond the facts she uncovered. She was also surprised at how many errors she discovered in the galley proofs. These two things convinced Kerr that she should stick to fiction. However, in our interview she did confess to still being occasionally tempted to undertake a dual biography of two people as fascinating as Kate Smith and Bobby Fischer, for example. They were both obsessive, but in entirely different ways.

In 1967 Kerr published under her own name what she calls the "obligatory family novel that every young writer must get out of his/her system." She says it was a "terrible bomb called *Hometown,*" which appropriately got the most attention in upstate New York, where her relatives were busy getting it out of libraries and bookstores.

Kerr was almost to conclude that her own name was a jinx, but then she published a hardback under the name of Meaker with

Little, Brown; *Shockproof Sydney Skate*. It featured a teenager and became a Literary Guild alternate and a selection of the Book Find Club. The money from the paperback sale was enough to make Kerr begin thinking of buying her own house outside New York City.

Besides writing while she lived in the city, Kerr took courses at the New School, studying psychology, literature, political science, sociology, anthropology, and, of course, writing. As a student, she met famous New Yorkers, including Margaret Mead, and made friends with people she would not otherwise have had access to as a beginning writer. The friendship that most affected her life was one with professor Martha Wolfenstein, a psychoanalyst specializing in children and young adults. Wolfenstein encouraged Kerr to read Freud, Reik, Stekel, Kubie, Mahler, and Fromm, and to subscribe to psychology journals. Without identifying her patients, she talked with Kerr about many of their problems.

Kerr sees at least two major benefits from their close friendship. First, it saved her the time and cost of psychoanalysis because she absorbed much of the process through osmosis. And second, what she learned about psychology enhanced her writing. Vin Packer's books became "whydunits" instead of "whodunits." And because Kerr studied adolescent psychology and talked with Wolfenstein about her young patients, Kerr included young people in many of her stories. She liked to fictionalize actual crimes—for example, the Emmet Till "Wolf Whistle" murder of a young black boy in Mississippi. Although her stories were intended for adult audiences, she told several of them from the viewpoint of a teenager; in the 1960s another good friend would keep reminding Kerr of this while encouraging her to try writing for young people.

This friend was Louise Fitzhugh, author of the ground-breaking children's book *Harriet the Spy* published in 1964. (Kerr refers to *Harriet the Spy* as a young adult book, but teachers and critics are more likely to think of it as an older children's book—something for fourth, fifth, and sixth graders.) What was unusual about *Harriet the Spy* was that it brought modern realism to children's literature. It features a girl who is so intriguing and funny that it disproves the old adage that boys won't read books about girls. The same observation would later be made about Kerr's books, but for a long time Kerr resisted Fitzhugh's suggestion to write for young people because it seemed to her that Fitzhugh was forced to talk down to her audience in *Harriet the Spy*. Kerr couldn't see herself writing in that limited fashion, but she kept Fitzhugh's advice in the back of her mind and regularly read books written for young people. Nothing clicked until she read Paul Zindel's *The Pigman*. She loved that book and wanted to write one just as good.

Kerr had been touched by the social turmoil of the sixties, especially the death of Martin Luther King, Jr. Wanting to contribute somehow to improving social and educational conditions for black people, she began serving in an experimental writers-in-the-schools program. One day a month she would go to Commercial Manhattan Central High School on 42d Street where she would endeavor in English classes to get students interested in writing. The students worked half a day and came to school half a day. She says "They were wild, unruly, wonderful kids who didn't give a fig for reading, but who responded to writing assignments with great vigor and originality." As part of the program, stories and poems that the students wrote were published in a mimeographed magazine. The most popular writer was a very fat black girl nicknamed Tiny who wrote imaginative grotesque stories. In one of them, a woman went swimming in the Hudson River and accidentally swallowed some strange eggs that were in the water. She subsequently gave birth to a mass of red snakes.

Kerr soon received a visit from Tiny's mother, who came to complain about Kerr encouraging her daughter to write "weird." As Kerr talked to the woman, and over the next few months as she got to know Tiny better, she found out that Tiny's mother spent most of her time working with her church to aid drug addicts. Every afternoon Tiny would go home to an empty apartment where she would eat snacks and watch television until her mother came home for supper. After dinner, which was the highlight of Tiny's day, the mother would go back to the church, and Tiny would again watch television and eat until she fell asleep. She was becoming enormous. Kerr says the mother was completely unaware that while she was putting out the fire across the street, her own house was burning.

Inspired by this mother-daughter relationship, Kerr finally wrote her first YA novel, *Dinky Hocker Shoots Smack!* Kerr changed the girl's color and her social status to one that she could write about more comfortably, but she kept the basic characters of a do-gooder mother and a daughter desperately in need of some of that good-doing.

Kerr offered *Dinky Hocker* to Harper and Row because they published Louise Fitzhugh's *Harriet the Spy,* and Fitzhugh was enthusiastic over Ursula Nordstrom as an editor who respected writers and their opinions. The company happily accepted Kerr's first YA novel and assigned Nordstrom as her editor. When Nordstrom retired, Kerr went on to work with Charlotte Zolotow and Robert O. Warren.

In *ME ME ME ME ME* and other places, Kerr has talked about the thrill of making the first big sale to *Ladies' Home Journal.* When asked if the publication of *Dinky Hocker* was a comparable pleasure, she responded "Not at all. It was a big disappointment." Editor Ursula Nordstrom had a way of making authors feel excited about whatever they did, but Kerr received only $2,000 from the 1972 hardback sales. She was accustomed to receiving between fifteen and twenty thousand dollars for a book. Even though she had already started *If I Love You, Am I Trapped Forever?* she was about to decide that writing for young people was a luxury that she could not afford. Then the money from the paperback sale came through, and Kerr was pleasantly surprised to find that "this little indulgence, this sideline" could actually make money.

She combined her profits with those from the paperback sale of *Shockproof Sydney Skate* and moved from New York City to Long Island, buying a house in East Hampton. In spite of what sounds like a bad luck address—a dead-end street named Deep Six Drive—Kerr's East Hampton home proved to be a good luck charm both for her and for hundreds of thousands of young readers. Since 1973, she has happily lived and worked in East Hampton writing books for young adults. Some of her most credible characters have been inspired by neighborhood teenagers, and several of her imaginative plots had their beginnings in some incident or activity that Kerr observed in her new hometown.

When she left New York City, Kerr missed the everyday contact she had with writers, and so in East Hampton she established a writers' workshop in a community center. It is a nonprofit undertaking with the fees that people pay going to a scholarship fund for disadvantaged students. The workshop meets once a week for twelve-week terms in the fall and spring. There are twenty members, including people in their twenties and their seventies. The group has been meeting for three years, and many are repeaters working on novels. Kerr enjoys the mix of people whose occupations range from bartender to minister, retired editor, teacher, and realtor.

The twenty years that Kerr spent in New York City as a professional writer for adults gave her a unique preparation for her second career as a writer for teenagers. In some ways her writing in 1952 does not seem so different from her writing in 1972; for example, Patrick Henry Casebolt, "an enormous, redheaded, freckle-faced ruffian . . . about to burst out of his gold braided jacket," bears a striking surface resemblance to P. John Knight in *Dinky Hocker Shoots Smack!* P. John was "a fat boy . . . nearly six feet, with red hair, freckles and red-apple cheeks, and he weighed around 220 pounds." However, looks aren't everything, and what P. John Knight has that Patrick Henry Casebolt does not have is depth. The same can be said for the book compared to the short story.

The story is entertaining and fun to read, but there's very little left to think about afterwards. In contrast, *Dinky Hocker Shoots Smack!* is entertaining reading for 190 pages, compared to five for the story, and at the end of the novel there is food for thought. Kerr's years of studying psychology, combined with her close friendship with a children's psychiatrist, gave her a background from which to create unusual but believable characters. Those years also gave her the empathy and imagination needed to glimpse an intriguing situation and then to play out the hidden parts in her own mind. The miscellaneous classes she took at the New School, the interesting people she met, and the books and journals she read gave her a wealth of knowledge from which she could select that information most likely to generate the intellectual curiosity that Kerr wants to share with young people. Her New York City years also helped her develop writing stamina. Between 1972 and 1985, no one else matched her record of twelve critically acclaimed and popular books for young adults.

Probably most important of all is the skill that Kerr developed. Writing teachers promise students that if they write seriously for at least an hour a day, they will eventually succeed. During her New York City years, Kerr averaged four or five hours a day doing a kind of writing that has several similarities to writing for young adults. Readers of suspense novels are like teen readers in wanting a quick, tight story that they can get into immediately. And because the plots from one book to another are similar, they want the stories enlivened with some unusual details and characters. The apparent ease with which Kerr transferred her talents from writing adult suspense stories to writing young adult problem novels with romantic and often humorous overtones exemplifies the truthfulness of the Alexander Pope quotation that the English teacher in Kerr's *Little Little* posts on the blackboard:

> True ease in writing comes from art, not chance.
> As those move easier who have learn'd to dance.

If I Love You, Am I Trapped Forever?

2. The Storyteller

In her autobiographical *ME ME ME ME ME—Not a Novel,* Kerr writes

What's going on in the world is secondary to what's going on in high school, for in those vulnerable teen years high school *is* the world. There . . . the idea of winning and losing starts taking shape, of being in or out, part of the crowd, or an outsider. . . . There, adults other than parents become role models or enemies or objects of ridicule. . . . And with all that is going on, there are changes going on at home, as kids begin to see things they hadn't noticed before: the way their parents get along, or don't, the way their own brothers and sisters are coping.

This is the raw material from which Kerr has fashioned the dozen novels described below. Taken as a body of literature, they have placed her among the most highly acclaimed contemporary writers for young people. Characteristics of her writing that can best be illustrated through examples from more than one book will be discussed in chapters 3 and 4.

Dinky Hocker Shoots Smack!

Dinky Hocker Shoots Smack! was M. E. Kerr's first book for young adults. It is still her most popular and in some ways her best. It begins with Tucker Woolf's father advising him not to tell people he lives in Brooklyn, but in Brooklyn *Heights,* "Believe me, Tucker, you'll make a better impression." Making a good impression is very important to Tucker's father, which is why Tucker feels sorry for him—it's hard to make a good impression when you've just been fired.

Tucker's father has been a fund-raiser for charitable organizations and small colleges. When he loses his job, the family moves from Manhattan to Brooklyn Heights, and Tucker's mother goes to work as a writer/editor for *Stirring Romances*. (Tucker is supposed to say she works for Arrow Publications.) The first night in Brooklyn Heights, Tucker finds an abandoned calico kitten hiding under an old Chevrolet. He adopts the cat and names it Ralph Nader in honor of the man "who had done his own time under Chevrolets," but then the cat turns out to be a female and so Tucker drops the "Ralph."

As the weeks drag on and Mr. Woolf does not get a new job, he becomes increasingly nervous. He also becomes allergic to cats so that Tucker has to give Nader away. In keeping with the local custom, Tucker puts a sign on a tree:

DO YOU FEEL UNWANTED, IN THE WAY, AND THE CAUSE OF EVERYONE'S MISERY? ARE YOU TALKED ABOUT BEHIND YOUR BACK AND PLOTTED AGAINST? THEN YOU KNOW HOW I FEEL. I AM A CALICO KITTEN PUTTING MYSELF UP FOR ADOPTION. I HAVE ALREADY BEEN SPAYED BY DR. WASSERMAN OF HICKS STREET, AND I AM IN GOOD CONDITION PHYSICALLY. MENTALLY I AM ON A DOWNER, THOUGH, UNTIL I CAN RELOCATE. IF YOU KNOW HOW A LOSER FEELS AND WANT TO HELP, CALL MAIN 4–8415.

Into the picture comes 5′4″, 165-pound Susan (known as Dinky) Hocker, who adopts Nader and immediately gives the cat her own problem of overeating. Tucker, who visits Nader at Dinky's house, is worried and depressed at how fat and lethargic Nader becomes. As Tucker's mother observes, "Somehow, you identify with that cat, and I don't see why. You've never been a stray. You've always been loved. . . . Why all the concern over this animal?"

Through his concern for Nader, Tucker gets acquainted with Dinky's family: a successful lawyer father who pays little attention to his family; one of the most insensitive mothers in all of young adult literature; a cousin named Natalia Line, who has just been released from a school for mentally disturbed teenagers; and various walk-ins that Dinky's do-gooder mother tries to help recover from their addictions and personal problems.

Tucker develops a crush on Dinky's cousin. So he can date Natalia, he fixes Dinky up with P. John Knight, another "fatty" who turns out to have much more in common with Dinky than a weight problem. Everything that Dinky's liberal parents approve of and believe in, P. John makes fun of. Finally they forbid Dinky to associate with P. John. Life gets worse and worse for Dinky until in desperation she does a terrible thing. While Mrs. Hocker is being honored at a community banquet for her work with drug addicts, Dinky paints the message, "Dinky Hocker Shoots Smack" on sidewalks, curbstones, walls, and doors of automobiles. As people file out of the awards ceremony there is no way they can miss it.

This gets the attention not only of the whole town, but also of Dinky's humiliated parents. However, it's up to Tucker to get them to understand that "People who don't shoot smack have problems too." Dinky wasn't being vindictive, she just needed to be listened to. When Tucker explains how thoughtless and cruel they have all been about P. John's friendship with Dinky, Mr. Hocker says, "It never amounted to much, after all."

"If it wasn't much," Tucker responds, "it was still all Susan ever had."

The book has a moderately happy ending. Tucker gets to have his cat back when his father gets a new job at half his old salary and discovers that he wasn't allergic to cats but to being out of work. Tucker's mother enrolls in law school; Natalia goes back to her special school for the summer, only this time as a helper; and Dinky and her mother and father go off to Europe for a real family trip. Tucker teases his parents that he is going to start overeating so he can get a trip to Europe, but they just laugh and say if he can get fat on his own cooking (he inherited the job of cooking when his mother entered law school) then he will deserve something special.

When Kerr wrote this book she was living in her apartment in Brooklyn Heights. Since she was near the courts, she was surrounded by lawyers and their families. This is why she chose to make Dinky's father a lawyer and why she thought of showing how Tucker's mother had ambitions of her own by having her go to law school. Kerr said that she watched dozens of such women go by her apartment building on their way to Brooklyn Law College. They were "much longer in the tooth" than typical college coeds and were obviously weighed down by family responsibilities as well as their law books.

The contrast between Tucker's mother and Dinky's mother is an example of one of Kerr's favorite techniques: setting up contrasting sets of characters in order to give readers more to think about. A student at Arizona State University described this show-both-sides approach by writing that

Tucker's parents weren't the perfect, all-knowing "Ward and June" of *Leave It to Beaver* fame nor were they the insensitive, closed-mind types that Paul Zindel created in *The Pigman*. They had a human warmth about them, and they tried—though not always successfully—to communicate with Tucker. They were the antithesis of the Hocker family where the parents—especially the mother—were so self-centered that at the end of the story I wondered if they really went to Europe for Dinky's sake or if Mrs. Hocker just wanted to get away from all the embarrassment surrounding the awards ceremony.

Another character brought into the story for contrast is the conservative P. John Knight, who serves as a foil to highlight the sameness of everyone else's liberal attitudes. P. John is admittedly an unrealistic exaggeration, but Kerr nevertheless deserves credit for finding so clever a way to shine a spotlight on the ridiculousness of extreme and unbending attitudes. That she does it and leaves readers smiling is all the better.

For pure hilarity few scenes rival her description of the evening of 10 December when P. John and Tucker take Dinky and Natalia to a dance. It begins with P. John arriving at Tucker's house, where everyone is working to prepare for the opening of the Help Yourself health food store that is going to be Mr. Woolf's new career. P. John nods his head "in that old wiser-than-all-the-world way" and says "You'll probably attract a lot of radicals." Then he goes on to explain that such people are often health nuts and vegetarians. For examples he cites Hitler and George Bernard Shaw, hastening to explain that Hitler was an exception because most such people "are weak-sister socialists like Shaw." When the amazed Mr. Tucker says, "I suppose you prefer Hitler," P. John says that he doesn't agree with Hitler all down the line, but at least "he didn't cozy up to the Communists like a lot of jelly-spined liberals."

At Dinky's house, P. John makes an equally startling impression on Dinky's parents. When Mr. Hocker hands over money for taxi fare because he doesn't think the subway is safe for coming home after the dance, P. John hands it back with the statement that he's one of the few New Yorkers not on the dole. When Mr. Hocker wants to check watches as he instructs the boys to get the girls home by twelve, P. John says "I don't own a watch anymore. A mugger relieved me of it in September, no doubt so he could report to the unemployment office in time to sign for his check."

The evening goes on like this so that by the end, Tucker is perspiring "worse than a Rose Bowl tackle on New Year's Eve." He has also decided that he is boring, a failure on the dating scene, obnoxious and bumptious, and just generally socially inadequate. That the beautiful Natalia still likes him is enough to warm the hearts of insecure readers everywhere. One of the strengths of Kerr's books is that she shows readers that there is room for the less-than-perfect, for those who aren't blessed with the unlimited self-confidence that pours out from most mass media presentations of the great American dream.

It is not surprising that *Dinky Hocker Shoots Smack!* received good reviews in practically every library or school-related publication. The story is well developed, the plot and characters original and interesting, and the dialogue warm and witty. Kerr must have been amused at those reviewers who praised it as an "impressive first book."

What makes *Dinky Hocker* so popular are the wonderfully fresh and believable details: the description of Nader in her "calorie-drugged sleep," Dinky dressed in her father's old tweed vest worn over a T-shirt with green cotton pajama bottoms and old tennis socks, and the way the Hocker's Christmas dinner progressed from an elegant holiday occasion to a shambles. Most diet-conscious teenagers have used Dinky's rationalizations and tricks, only not to the same extent. Many young people, probably more today than when the book was written, identify with the hard-nosed line that P. John takes, and they smile knowingly about Marcus and the contradictions that he mouths about pot. Because they have relatives who sometimes need help, they are interested in how the families relate to Dinky's cousin Natalia and to Tucker's Uncle Guy. But most of all they are drawn in by the wonderful lines that Kerr puts into her characters' mouths, as when P. John predicts Dinky's breakdown by wryly commenting that "Fish die belly-upward, too," when Tucker explains that *ass* is a bad word because when "they made the rules, they decided any part of your body that isn't supposed to show isn't supposed to be called by a slang name," and when Dinky tells the true story of John Merrick and Tucker tells the false "true confession" that his mother made up for her magazine about the hospital nurse who for twenty years switched around the newborn babies in her care.

The weaknesses in *Dinky Hocker Shoots Smack!* stem from the same root as the strengths: Kerr's exuberance. Her exaggerations make for entertaining reading, but it's a bit hard to believe that Dinky would or could have painted her message so that it showed "no matter what street you turned down." If she really painted it on car doors as well as sidewalks and walls, then the dire consequences should have at least been mentioned.

Credibility is also stretched by the interrelationships of such a cast of characters. Certainly there are people as troubled and as eccentric as each of Kerr's characters, but they usually find ways to avoid dealing with each other. Putting them all together so they could contribute to solving each others' problems results in an ending that is a bit too pat. Nevertheless, readers are left with new ideas about schools, family relationships, emotional disturbances, women's roles, and controlling one's appetites, whether for food or drugs.

If I Love You, Am I Trapped Forever?

Alan Bennet goes against his grandfather's advice when he uses a first-person point of view to write *If I Love You, Am I Trapped Forever?* His grandfather, who also wanted to be a writer but ended up running a department store, tells Alan that writing in the first person is like painting with watercolors—only geniuses and small children can do it well. Ordinary mortals end up writing self-involved word-salads that no one but relatives will read.

Alan says it's really not his story he's telling but that of Duncan Stein, a Jewish boy who moves to Cayuta, New York, at the beginning of both boys' senior year. The new boy acquires the nickname Doomed because he looks like a loser, going bald and wearing funny little glasses. His parents have come to establish Rushing Brook Farm, also called Lushing Brook because it's a recovery place for alcoholics.

In his own words, Alan is "*the* most popular boy in school." Out of modesty, he tells readers to simply take out a piece of paper and write down their idea of a "very handsome, very cool guy who's dynamite," and then think of Alan. Alan has an equally impressive girlfriend named Leah. They begin going steady the same day Alan first speaks to Doomed, inviting him to go out for the basketball team. When Doomed says "he doesn't go that route" (he's not a jock), Alan persists by asking Doomed if he's ever heard of Hank Greenberg, Sandy Koufax, or Mark Spitz.

"Two were baseball players, one was a swimmer. So What?"

Frustrated by Doomed's lack of perception, Alan says, "Well, they're also of the Jewish persuasion. The fact shouldn't discourage anyone from going out for sports."

The nonplussed Doomed looks through Alan and says he isn't of any persuasion except "maybe the isolationist persuasion."

This conversation reappears twice in the story, first when Alan repeats it to his girlfriend Leah and her twin sister, Sophie, who scoffs at Alan and asks how he would like it if she offered to be his friend because she "had other friends whose fathers had deserted their mothers before they were born, too." This is what happened to Alan, and he takes advantage of being insulted in this way to get a little extra sympathy.

The next time Alan's memorable conversation appears is when Alan goes with his mother, the official Finger Lakes Friends (FLF) greeter to welcome the Steins into the community. Mrs. Stein asks Alan if he knows anything about tennis, because they plan to put in a tennis court for the "guests." She cheerfully acknowledges that Mr. Stein isn't any better than his son at sports. "You're right Alan—Jews aren't great jocks." Alan is shocked that she had heard about his conversation with Doomed and he stammers out a denial. But when he gets to the part about "those of the Jewish persuasion," Mrs. Stein breaks out giggling—in a nice way. Before Alan and his mother leave, he is very much taken with the attractive Mrs. Stein. But whenever she mentions her son, he thinks it's "like the Mona Lisa suddenly looking down from her frame and launching into a discussion of the local Chevrolet dealer, the Avon lady, or the bowlegged boy who lived across the street."

From here the plot of the story takes off like a roller coaster, but because readers have had time to get comfortably seated they hang on and enjoy the ride. It's only afterward that they look back and wonder if so many things could have happened to change so many lives in one short school year. Doomed reverses his negative image, becoming the most sought-after boy in school through founding and editing a newspaper called *Remote*. It is filled with obscure but very romantic stories and want ads that eventually result in Duncan and Leah (Alan's "terrific" girlfriend) falling in love. Alan's long absent father decides that he wants to get to know his "son" and invites Alan to New York City for a less-than-successful weekend visit. At the airport, Alan sees his alcoholic football coach with Catherine Stein, and on the bus ride home from Syracuse to Cayuta he sits by the weeping Mrs. Stein, who pledges him to secrecy about the trip. This little conspiracy and the great sadness that he perceives increases the feelings that he already has for her. By spring he is visiting Mrs. Stein every Thursday afternoon when Duncan has to stay at school for yearbook staff meetings. They share their broken hearts, although his is the only one they ever talk about. Alan compares the strength of Catherine Stein, who chose to stay, with the weakness of his father, who chose to leave. At the end of the school year when Alan is deciding that he loves her so much that he will not go to college but will stay in Cayuta to be near her, he learns that Mrs. Stein—now that she is sure that Duncan is going to "make it"— has gone to join the alcoholic football coach who left town in the middle of the year.

As Alan realizes, when he spends the evening of the junior prom by himself on the beach drinking wine and reading Dostoyevski, while Duncan takes Leah to the dance, he has more or less traded places with Doomed. It is from the pain of this year's experiences that he writes the book.

Young adult author Richard Peck has pointed out that the teenagers who are readers of books such as his and Kerr's come from the great middle group of students, not the extremes on either end. Students at the lower end—the drop-outs, the drug addicts, the losers—do not know how to read. At the upper end, the students like Alan—the student body presidents, the newspaper editors, the football players, and the cheerleaders—are involved in so many projects that they have no time for leisure reading. Nevertheless, it is the extremes whose stories are the most interesting, and so these are the people who get written about. However, Peck explains that when he writes these stories about the extremes, he always keeps in mind that his readers are most likely going to be from the middle.

Kerr has not articulated this, but the plot of *If I Love You, Am I Trapped Forever?* shows that she understands it. It is very satisfying for typical students to see how fast a boy like Alan can topple from his perch and how through cleverness and hard work, as opposed to natural born good looks, someone like Duncan Stein can lift himself to the top.

Another positive aspect of *If I Love You, Am I Trapped Forever?* is the portrayal of some good mother-son relationships, although Kerr goes too far when she asks readers to believe that Alan would miss football practice, or that his mother would ask him to, so that he could assist her in welcoming new families to Ca-

yuta. Alan's friendship with Duncan's mother is a more troublesome part of the plot. It can be looked on as the one unlikely but
necessary element to make a good story, but the tranquil Thursday afternoons that Alan spends with her simply do not fit with
the other details Kerr presents. Catherine Stein is worried over
whether Duncan is going to "make it"; she is not physically close
to the man she loves and who desperately needs her; she has her
own husband to worry about, and she has responsibilities connected with Rushing Brook and the need for a unified family appearance. In the midst of all this, few women would be able to
concentrate on a friendship with a high school senior, even if they
were flattered by his obvious devotion and touched by his broken
heart.

It is hard to decide whether the abundance of literary references in *If I Love You, Am I Trapped Forever?* should be counted
as a strength or a weakness. Quotations from Petrarch, Dostoyevski, Tennessee Williams, and O. Henry along with references to
Thomas Wolfe, J. D. Salinger, and Dante move the plot along in
an interesting way, but because there are so many of them as well
as several literary pieces from Duncan's *Remote* newspaper, they
sound a bit forced.

Also forced are such coincidences as Alan's seeing the coach's
little blue Triumph parked at the airport and then Alan and the
weeping Mrs. Stein having adjacent seats on the bus trip home.
Kerr defends her use of these coincidences by having Alan argue
that "They say there are some things you can't put in a novel
because they don't ring true, even though they are." Alan's English teacher, Mrs. Tompkins, has told him that to be believable
fiction must "avoid all life's bizarre coincidences." Alan asks Mrs.
Tompkins if when he writes an autobiographical novel he has to
discard "actual happenings which seem unreal," and she comes
back with "all you can do is try and see if they come across in a
believable way."

Fortunately, most of Kerr's readers are so caught up in the story
that they do not stop to question her coincidences. They are grap-
pling with the bigger question that she forces them to think

about: If you have good intentions, is it wrong to turn someone else's world upside down to fill your own needs?

The Son of Someone Famous

There are enough unlikely coincidences in *The Son of Someone Famous* to sink a book three times its size. What keeps it afloat is the characterization of Brenda Belle Blossom. This vulnerable teenager is presented with such touching believability that one is led to suspect that there must be a lot of the teenage Marijane Meaker inside of her.

One of the arguments that Brenda Belle has with her mother about the value of humor appears almost word-for-word as an argument between Marijane and her mother in the autobiographical *ME ME ME ME ME*. And the relationship that Marijane has with her boyfriend in *ME ME ME ME ME* (they were affectionate only in public) resembles the one that Brenda Belle has with Adam Blessing, the title character. Brenda and Adam are indeed good friends, but the romantic part of their friendship is purely for the sake of public appearances. Brenda Belle thinks it will please her mother if she goes steady, and Adam is amenable to the idea of fitting in by having a girlfriend even it if isn't Christine Cutler, about whom he writes:

There is a Christine Cutler in every town. It wouldn't be enough to say she was blonde and blue-eyed. The Christine Cutlers of the world can have any color hair or eyes—they are still all alike. If you had to choose only one word to describe them, it would be Special. They are The Most Beautiful, The Most Popular, The Most Likely to Succeed; and they are *It*.

Superficially, the plot centers around Brenda Belle and Adam's sort-of romance, but it is really the story of their achieving the kind of maturity they need to relate to the adults in their lives at an appropriate level of independence. The story begins in the cold weeks before Christmas of Brenda Belle's sixteenth winter when she is worried that she is changing into a boy because instead of growing breasts she is growing "a small fringe of hair" above her upper lip and telephone operators make remarks like "Just one moment, sir." She is consumed with two ideas: either ending it all or running away to New York City, where no one will know her. What she does instead is sneak into the drugstore during the off-hours and ask the druggist, Mr. Corps, for "something called Hairgo." He thinks she says "Hairdo," and then when he gets the word straight, he still doesn't understand, and she has to clarify her request by explaining she wants a depilatory.

She is horribly embarrassed when she discovers that the new boy in town, Adam Blessing, sitting in the back booth of the drugstore, has overheard her request. For his benefit she adds, "I have a great deal of unsightly hair to remove from the soles of my feet."

Adam isn't at all embarrassed by this conversation, and he joins in with his own witticisms. The conversation is a delightful bit of give-and-take, far too clever to have occurred spontaneously. Nevertheless, it makes readers laugh; and they can have fun imagining themselves carrying on such clever dialogue. Afterwards, Adam writes a line in his journal that is probably evidence of wish fulfillment on the part of Marijane Meaker as well as the bright and clever girls who are attracted to her books: "I like funny girls. I always have." Adam's reason is that funny girls are so much easier to talk to.

Adam's mother died when he was a baby. His father is a prominent politician or diplomat, sort of like Henry Kissinger at the peak of his days in shuttle diplomacy. Adam has been expelled from numerous boarding schools. His explanation is that he cracks under the pressure to keep up the family image of super success. His father scoffs and says that's an excuse, not a reason. As a last resort, Adam comes to Storm, Vermont, to live with his maternal grandfather, a retired veterinarian who is also the town drunk. Adam takes his grandfather's name so he won't be recognized.

The coincidences start piling up when Adam's former stepmother, a has-been movie star, decides to come for Christmas and is recognized by faithful fans, namely Brenda's mother and aunt. She is soon followed to town by the starlet who is aspiring to become Adam's next stepmother. Adam is the one who has to cope with her suicide attempt when she figures out that his famous father is trying to ditch her. And finally Brenda learns the shocking true story that Adam's natural mother was killed when she was running away with Christine Cutler's father.

Brenda keeps this to herself, but she's not so quiet about the fact that she's beginning to see past the sequestered little world of teenage values in Storm, Vermont. As part of her expanded horizons she goes bird watching with Milton Merrensky. He's not the typical teenage hero and as Brenda Belle's mother sighs, "I wouldn't be interested in him for a boyfriend." Brenda Belle answers, "He wouldn't be interested in you for a girlfriend either." This is more than teenage insolence. It's an indication of Brenda Belle's newly earned independence of thought.

Kerr has a reverence for celebrities that comes through in this book in spite of its overt message that readers should not envy the rich and famous because their money cannot buy love. In *ME ME ME ME ME* Kerr makes fun of her mother and her aunt, who love Hollywood gossip and delight in getting celebrity autographs. Even though she is amused at their behavior, she apparently inherited their interest—so many of her books feature celebrities—but there is something about the way she presents these famous people that does not ring quite true. Mary Burns put her thumb squarely on the issue when she wrote in a review that the "incidents seem patched together from speculation about a life style sensed but not experienced."[3] If it were only Adam's father who was the celebrity, that would not be so crucial to the story, because he never actually appears. But when his former wife and his girlfriend, both Hollywood stars, come to town the story comes close to disintegrating. Their actions are so clichéd, especially those of the girlfriend, that readers can hardly care about them.

Nevertheless, Kerr deserves credit for at least bringing up a topic that few other writers have dared to approach: the sexuality of a parent. Adam is embarrassed at the women his father dates and the snide remarks made in gossip columns showing him as a dirty old man. Adam is humble about criticizing because he thinks his father has earned the right to behave anyway he wants while Adam hasn't done enough in life to have the right to question. Readers know better.

At the end of the book, Adam journeys to California, where his former stepmother and his grandfather Blessing have moved to run an unconventional ice cream store. Because of his year in Storm, Adam comes to see his father in a softer light. After learning how his own mother lost her life, Adam can appreciate why his father "never drops his guard, or trusts, or lets himself become too seriously involved with anyone. . . . It is possible that all the hurt has made him so good at what he does; it is equally possible that such a man is only good at what he does, and not good at all at the things most men do easily."

Either way, Adam has also come to realize that he has his own life to live and people to meet and things to do that will have nothing to do with his father and his mother. Things are going to happen solely to him and it's time he get ready.

Is That You, Miss Blue?

Is That You, Miss Blue? is an autobiographical novel based upon the story of Kerr's leaving Auburn, New York, after her second year in high school and going away to boarding school in Virginia. In the novel, the school is called Charles School, while in real life it was Stuart Hall near Staunton, Virginia.

Fourteen-year-old Flanders Brown tells the story beginning with her train trip from New York to Virginia. She meets an "old" student, Carolyn Cardmaker, who feels qualified to expound on everything and everyone. As Carolyn explains, she has a high I.Q. and she's also a P.K. (preacher's kid), which means she is a category #1 student: bright and pitiful. Carolyn says that all the students fit into one of four categories. Besides the bright and black, oriental, migrant worker, etc., categories there are category #2 girls, whose social-climbing parents like the prestige of having a daughter away at boarding school. Category #3 girls are in the way because their parents are getting divorced or have more exciting things to do than raise children. Category #4 girls are "out of the ordinary," handicapped or exceptionally bright or beautiful, etc. Carolyn decides that Flanders is a #3, and midway though the book Flanders almost agrees.

Part of the appeal of the book is that Flanders satisfies some of the curiosity that readers feel as they look forward to moving out of their parents' homes: "I felt a rush of loneliness, the type that comes for a second or two like great punches in the stomach and then goes without doing any damage, except to keep you ever alert to the idea that your life has changed completely, overnight." Surrounded by strangers she's not sure she will ever care about, Flanders envies Cardmaker because she appears to be "so wrapped up in everything and everyone." Flanders soon learns that she is suffering from misplaced envy—a not uncommon occurrence at Charles School.

Flanders has asthma, and her roomate, Agnes, is deaf. They are put in an out-of-the-way dorm so that if they make noises in the night they won't awaken the other girls. Miss Ernestine Blue is assigned to be the faculty "pal" living on the same floor with them. She is a woman who Flanders senses needs protection. In an article for the *ALAN Review* ("Feed the Wonder," 1982), Kerr described a teacher she had a crush on back in Auburn, New York. There's a lot of this teacher in Miss Blue, who in Flanders's words, "had the effect on most people of embarrassing them, as in the sentence 'I was embarrassed for her.'" In class, Miss Blue is a wonderful teacher, but personally she is as mysterious as the scientific puzzles that she explores with students. She is "only around forty, not old and strange from living too long, but strange for some other reason." Cardmaker explains to Flanders,

"She can hear Jesus. Far out."
"What do you mean she can hear Jesus far out? Far out where?"
"I mean it's far out that she can hear Jesus. It's Ding-A-Ling City."

Flanders's first experience with Miss Blue's religious nature comes when she goes into their shared bathroom and finds hanging on the wall a "crown-of-thorn-type" picture of Jesus and the verse

O bleeding face, O face divine,
Be love and adoration thine.

If someone her own age had been with her, they would have collapsed on the floor in a giggling fit—"not that the idea of Christ's bleeding face was funny, but things out of context often seem preposterous." But since Flanders is facing this alone, except for Miss Blue waiting for a comment, her reaction is one of self-consciousness. She resents that Miss Blue has been foisted off on her and she knows that to contend with the situation, she will "make it all a joke, one big laugh to share with everyone."

Dual feelings run throughout the book with Flanders making fun of Miss Blue and then feeling guilt, shame, and protectiveness. When Miss Blue is dismissed from her teaching position— even a church-sponsored school like Charles can't cope with someone like Miss Blue—Flanders and her friends conspire to soften the blow. But in spite of their efforts, when Flanders gets home for Christmas where everything should be just fine, she suddenly gets "the loneliest feeling in the world," and as her father and grandmother shout "Merry Christmas!" she whispers into the storm, "Miss Blue, are you okay?" She knows the answer is no.

When Kerr was young, she hated to read historical fiction. This is why she translated her 1940s school experience at Stuart Hall into a contemporary setting, but it caused her a problem that she did not think about until she received a letter from a recent graduate of a boarding school. The woman said that today's boarding schools are not nearly as strict as the one Kerr presented. Kerr acknowledged this as justified criticism.

Fortunately the focus of *Is That You, Miss Blue?* is not on the boarding school experience as much as it is on people's inner feelings, and those are quite the same in the 1980s as in the 1940s. A reviewer in *Best Sellers* described the value of the book nicely when she said that what Kerr does is to "dig deep and scurry around in the loneliest, saddest corners of a reader's soul."[4] In doing this, Kerr also manages to show readers that religion can mean very different things to different people and that the way people react to external events is often shaped by their internal struggles.

One might quibble with a few of Kerr's final editorial decisions, such as contriving to teach Flanders and readers much more than deaf Agnes could ever express orally. Kerr has a breeze scatter Agnes's papers around the room. As Flanders picks them up, she reads a letter Agnes has written but not yet mailed explaining why she is so insulted to be fixed up with a blind boy. Kerr manages to teach us a lesson, but she creates an unconvincing scene in order to do so. Similarly, if Kerr were writing Miss Blue's story in 1985 rather than in 1975, she would probably have decided against the little joke whereby Cardmaker remembers her phone number 324-2455 with the story "three times a twenty-four-year-old girl was raped by a twenty-four-year-old boy and a fifty-five-year-old man." The joke sounds more forced than most of Kerr's humor, and feminists, with whose philosophies Kerr usually agrees, have made a persuasive argument that rape is not a joking matter.

Love Is a Missing Person

Love Is a Missing Person has been singularly ignored by the prize givers. This does not mean it is a "bad" book; it is just not quite such a "good" book as some of the others. When Lillian Gerhardt reviewed it in *School Library Journal,*[5] she said it was "as interesting as unfinished gossip." This description hints at the book's weakness as well as its strength. The weakness is that it tries to tell too many people's stories. The strength is that instead of looking at the most obvious aspects of these stories, Kerr zeroes in on parts that usually stay below the surface.

She got the idea for the book when she went to a high school football game in East Hampton. During halftime she watched a pretty blonde girl run up to the cheerleaders. Their greetings showed that they hadn't seen each other for some time. In her arms, the girl carried a baby wrapped in a blanket. Standing at some distance behind her was a tall black boy. As the girl unfolded the blanket for the cheerleaders to see, Kerr caught a glimpse of a tiny black baby.

When Kerr said something to a nearby friend about the inevitability of intermarriage, her friend responded with, "Ah, but that's not the real story. The real story is the anger that black girls here have," because the white girls are taking "their men." Black sports heroes date white girls, but there is no comparable group of white boys dating black girls. Kerr tried to bring this insight to a wider audience in *Love Is a Missing Person*.

One of Kerr's strengths is her ability to create characters with whom readers can identify, but in this book the characters are spread thin. Fifteen-year-old $uzy $lade, whose name gets written with dollar signs because of the wealth of her family, tells the story. But crowding her off the pages are various relatives and friends. First is her older sister Chicago, "an original" who roars into town on her motorcycle and then roars out taking with her a beautiful black athlete. This athlete happens to be the senior class valedictorian and, until Chicago arrives, the boyfriend of Suzy's black girlfriend and fellow worker at the town library.

Suzy's divorced mother and father also appear, and two-thirds of the way through the book, her father's new wife, a former cocktail waitress named Enid, enters the picture. There is a touching scene when Suzy makes her first visit to their house and gets an insight into the challenges facing this woman. Suzy notices *The International Thesaurus of Quotations* and on a page held open by a book of matches the note "Memorize for Suzy's visit." It is written next to the Charles Lamb quote about getting ideas from books that Enid had used so inappropriately the night before. Suzy presents Enid as a sympathetic character, but Suzy's mother describes her as a "redheaded creature with orange toenails" who thinks *Vogue* is a weekly and who calls her little dog "Fancy."

A quite separate story is that of Miss Gwendolyn Spring, the librarian who supervises Suzy and her friend. Miss Spring lives in the past dreaming about her World War II romance with Lester Quinn, who one afternoon appears at the library. Suzy is surprised that he is not "the baby-faced, innocent-eyed, laughing lieutenant" in the framed picture on Miss Spring's desk. He comes to borrow money, which to Suzy's surprise Miss Spring lends him and then explains, "Do you think his wanting a loan could puncture a delusion that has been in existence since the end of World War II?" Later she confides to Suzy, "I wasted myself in futile fantasy. I grew wrinkles dreaming. Wrinkles should come from living, not imagining that you are."

Miss Spring's story is perhaps the most intriguing in the book, but it gets overshadowed by the more recognizable stories of sibling rivalry, interracial loves and resentments, a wealthy older man marrying a sexy young woman he doesn't respect, and two teenagers running away as part of their rebellion against family and society. Authors sometimes say that once they have created their characters, the characters take over, writing their own stories and speaking in their own voices. It's almost eerie the way Miss Spring says to Suzy: "I don't give a tinker's dam, honey, what is going down the road right now. All I know is that I'm a car wreck smack-dab in the middle, broken and bleeding and, more's the pity, still drawing deep breaths. How many times am I going to be run over by the rest of you out driving in your big hurries?" Miss Spring isn't complaining to Suzy as much as she is to M. E. Kerr that the highway of this book is overcrowded with characters, and keeping them all moving in the direction of a unified plot is taking its toll.

Kerr said that *Love Is a Missing Person* was not welcomed by many teachers and parents although she has received positive letters from young readers familiar with problems of interracial dating. Apparently Kerr feels that adults rejected the book on the basis of its subject matter, which points to a troublesome area of book evaluation. When a book treats a controversial topic, it is almost impossible to separate a literary criticism of that book from readers' reactions to what they perceive as a social message. This is even more of a problem when books for young people are reviewed by adults because adults are naturally anxious that young readers grow up with the "right" attitudes, that is, the attitudes of the reviewer. This means that two reviewers might respond entirely differently to such scenes in *Love Is a Missing Person* as the one in which Roger's conciliatory uncle comes to talk to the Slades in hopes of making peace and the one in which the black girls wait for Chicago, hold her down, and cut off her hair. With scenes like this, it is impossible for critics to look purely at the "quality" of the writing because judging believable character development, consistent point of view, and authenticity of language is inevitably influenced by the background experiences of the reviewers.

It is probably just as impossible for writers not to be subconsciously influenced by their choice of subject matter. When Kerr wrote *Dinky Hocker Shoots Smack!* she changed her protagonist from a black girl because she did not feel qualified to write from a black viewpoint. Perhaps it was this same lack of confidence that made her crowd so many other stories into what started out as an exploration of relationships between black and white teenagers.

I'll Love You When You're More Like Me

I'll Love You When You're More Like Me is the story of Wallace Witherspoon Jr.'s life during the summer between his junior and senior years of high school. It begins and ends at almost the same place with Wally giddy with love (and lust) for Lauralei Rabinowitz. On the first page of the book, it's early spring and he and Lauralei are in the back of the family hearse—Wallace's father is a mortician—and he is whispering "I love you, I love you." Suddenly Lauralei sits up, reaches for her comb, and declares that this can't go on any longer because Wallace is not Jewish, he's shorter than she is, and he's going to be a mortician. Five months later, on the last page of the book, Wally catches up with Lauralei as she's leaving the school building. After small talk in which he finds that she's no longer going with the boy who had succeeded him and after she links her arm in his, he grandly announces that he's no longer going to be an undertaker.

"Marvelous," she says. "Super. . . . Now if you were two feet taller and your name was Witherstein, you'd be perfect!" Wally doesn't take her statement too seriously because as his Uncle Albert says, "You can't win them all." And after what Wally has been through he knows that anything might happen.

During the summer between Wally's school-year courtships of Lauralei, he finds himself "unofficially" engaged to Harriet Hren, who is shorter and prettier than Lauralei and also has some very good ideas for the mortuary business. "But Harriet was a math lesson and Lauralei was a whole course in Chemistry." That summer Wallace also becomes friends with Sabra St. Amour, a teenage soap-opera star who is suffering from an ulcer and has come to Seaville for a vacation while the grownups in her life figure out how to keep her both healthy and a star.

The other interesting character in the story is Wally's best friend, Charlie Gilhooley, who when he was sixteen began telling a few close associates that "he believed he preferred boys to girls." This shouldn't have been news to people who knew Charlie, "but honesty has its own rewards: ostracism and disgrace."

Wally's biggest problem is that he is his mortician father's only son and his father expects him to take over the family business. Wally hates the idea, especially the succession part, which makes his father's profession sound "like vampiricism which has to be passed on to each succeeding generation." All his life he has been teased with crude jokes about "just dying to see you," and with singing telephone calls: "The worms crawl in, the worms crawl out," etc. He used to console himself with the idea that these erstwhile friends would sooner or later be wheeled to the Witherspoon mortuary, but that wasn't very comforting when Wally remembered he was in line to be the next embalmer. Fortunately for Wally, parental pressure is relieved when his friend Charlie begins working at the mortuary.

Kerr makes life in the mortuary believable with homey details such as that an open coffin is a tempting napping place for the family cat and that what is served for dinner depends on whether or not there is "a guest." People do not want to smell corned beef and cabbage when they come to pay their last respects. Kerr may have drawn these effective details from her association with her high school boyfriend, Donald Dare, whose father ran a mortuary, as she describes in *ME ME ME ME ME*.

Some writers for young readers get their humor from consistently making adults look foolish. For the most part, Kerr avoids this; her protagonists make fun of each other as often as they do of grownups. Still, it may be especially satisfying to teenagers to read Wally's description of his boss at the soda shop as a "wraparound baldie" or to read how A. E. goes her mother one better when she is instructed to tell crank callers at the mortuary, "You are an ill person and you should see a doctor." A. E. says exactly this, and then when her mother smiles approvingly, she adds as a kicker, "And after you die from your illness, we'll be seeing you!"

Of all of Kerr's books, this is the one in which she tries to win the most laughs, as when Wally and Charlie are out with television star Sabra St. Amour. When Sabra doesn't like the hotdog at Dunn's, they tease her about going to the Waldorf Astoria for "creamed caviar over smashed brains" or to the Astor for "stuffed rooster under plexiglass." Then Wally shouts, "Waiter! Take back this aardvark nose, it's running," and Charlie adds, "Garcon! Remove this camel's eye, it's crying."

In spite of its situation-comedy approach, the book treats some serious topics: parental pressures, the price of fame, a mother who embarrasses her daughter with her sexual longings, and a likable young man who happens to be homosexual. Maybe it's because of Charlie's sexual preference that Kerr steers clear of the grimness that pervades such other YA books that touch on homosexuality as Lynn Hall's *Sticks and Stones,* John Donovan's *I'll Get There, It Better Be Worth the Trip,* and Isabelle Holland's *The Man without a Face.* Whereas these three books are controversial, Kerr's is not—probably because she disarms critics by making them smile. She manages to walk the thin line between laughing at Charlie and being sympathetically amused over his frustrations, as when Wally asks him how he can mourn the loss of a love he's never had, and he comes back with the logical answer, "It's all the harder."

Gentlehands

Kerr jokes about having a captive audience because students sometimes write and confide, as if it were a great compliment, that they were forced by an English teacher to read one of her books. If a particular title was assigned, chances are that it was *Gentlehands,* which is Kerr's most controversial but most intriguing book.

The book is unusual for its combination of an entertaining and light love story with a thought-provoking and fairly heavy "message." It starts at the beginning of summer with the kinds of problems that most high school kids are accustomed to thinking about: the social insecurities of wearing a Made-in-Korea orlon sweater when everyone else wears lamb's wool, falling in love with someone whose pool house is bigger than the house you live in, and suddenly looking at your family through new "grown-up" eyes and feeling ashamed.

Sixteen-year-old Buddy Boyle tells the story. He lives "in Seaville, New York, on a seedy half-acre lot up near the bay," while Skye, the girl he falls in love with, summers "on five oceanview acres at the other end of town." Buddy's dad is a police sergeant while Skye's dad is chairman of the board of Penn Industries. Buddy's only previous experience with Skye's kind of people was a trip with his mother to Montauk to meet "Grampa Trenker," the father she never knew. He lived in a huge house by the ocean and was "one of these foreign types with the classical music going and a lot of talk about his gardens." He seemed all right, but Buddy was eager to leave because his mother was so uncomfortable. She had been born in Germany and brought as an infant to the United States by her divorced mother. She resented that not until she was a grown woman had her father even written to inquire about

her; and now that he lived only twenty minutes away she chose
for the most part to ignore him. Her explanation for taking Buddy
to visit was so that he could see for himself that "he doesn't have
two heads or anything."

It's only when Buddy feels desperate to impress Skye that he
thinks of visiting his grandfather again. Skye invites Buddy to a
party at her house and afterwards she surprises him with a kiss
"just for the sweetest, shortest time," and then she steps away
and touches a button to the garage door, which rolls open so the
lights display six sleek cars, including a Rolls Royce and a Jensen.
Skye moves to the Jensen, which she calls The Jenny and asks,
"Want a lift somewhere, sailor? . . . Make it someplace special,
Buddy."

Buddy amazes himself by confidently saying "Montauk," and
then explaining that his grandfather lives there. Skye gives this
surprise her ultimate compliment: "Oh Buddy, that's subtle! I'm
going to like you, Buddy Boyle, I can tell."

The visit is such a success that both Buddy and his grandfather
acknowledge—and probably Skye recognizes—that Buddy is
"borrowing glory" by letting this sophisticated and elegant old
man make the impression on Skye that Buddy should have been
making with his own personality. But as Buddy philosophically
shrugs, "Thank God I had someone in my family to borrow glory
from."

By the end of the book, this borrowed glory almost turns into
borrowed infamy when it is revealed that Buddy's grandfather
was a Nazi war criminal and his wealth came from the melted-
down gold teeth and jewelry of Jewish victims. Kerr does not try
in this 135-page book to answer the questions about the Holocaust that the world has been struggling with for the past forty
years. What she does instead is make readers wonder about good
and evil and what outside appearances tell about inside courage
and beliefs.

Gentlehands was Kerr's easiest book to write. When she first
moved to East Hampton she lived next door to a seventeen-year-
old boy having his first love affair with one of the wealthy girls
whose families summered on the shore. The boy had just gotten

a new ten-speed bicycle while the girl had a new Porsche. She had gone to boarding schools in Europe while he went to the local high school. He would come to Kerr for advice on what clothes to wear and which fork to use first, agonizing over a hundred little details he had never thought about before.

That same summer Kerr was reading Howard Blum's book *WANTED: The Search for Nazis in America*. Blum's book and the experience with her neighbor came together so naturally that Kerr said it took her only three weeks to write *Gentlehands*. Kerr was not making the same kind of statement that Mrs. La Belle makes in *Little, Little* when she brags about writing her perfectly dreadful poem in a single afternoon. Instead, Kerr was marveling over a phenomenon that she hardly understood. She said it was as if she had a tape recorder in her head, and all she had to do was transcribe the story that someone else had put there.

Gentlehands became immediately controversial. Some people said it was anti-Semitic because the Nazi Grandpa Trenker was portrayed as much more appealing than another character, a Jewish writer devoting his life to hunting Nazis. Other people claimed that Trenker's switch from villain to hero lacked verisimilitude, while still others thought the topic inappropriate for young readers. Kerr was not surprised at the controversy; she had purposely set out to jar people's thinking. "Actually," she said, "Vietnam was as much in my mind as was World War II. As Americans we were in Vietnam, and I kept wondering were we all good people? Is evil conducted by someone next door or by someone so distant we don't recognize them?" She went on to say, "The fact that the boy turned his grandfather in was enough of a lesson for me."

Gentlehands is approaching *Dinky Hocker Shoots Smack!* as the most widely read of Kerr's books partly because it fits into course units on Holocaust literature, a popular reading topic in social studies and English classes. At 135-pages, *Gentlehands* may be the shortest book on a teacher's suggested reading list, and for young readers who have never thought about the Holocaust it is probably the easiest to accept. The critic who labeled the book a "slick little tale in which the Holocaust and Nazi exterminators become cheap devices to move the plot forward,"[6] was looking at the book from the wrong end of the telescope. Kerr's intention was to use the romantic elements to move readers to think about questions of cruelty and justice. She was following the well-established educational principle of starting at a student's level and then moving gradually on to higher levels of understanding.

Kerr's usual strength is her character development, but in *Gentlehands* the plot is the most interesting element. Buddy is the only memorable character; the others border on caricature. If after the excitement of her three-week writing marathon, Kerr had gone back and further developed each of the main characters, she may possibly have interrupted the straightforward flow of the story. Nevertheless, *Gentlehands* would have been a better book if Kerr had taken a second look and revised a few of the plotting devices she relied on in her rush to get on with the story. For example, the ending is weakened by Buddy's return to his grandfather's house to find "things strewn everywhere, as though someone had been on a frantic search for something." Books and tapes were out of the cases; drawers emptied onto the Oriental rug; cups, dishes, and silverware spread out on the kitchen floor, drapes torn from the windows, and wall pictures either crooked or taken down. When Buddy comes in and surveys the destruction, he hears what he thinks is music and a closet door closing.

Supposedly all of this purposeful-looking damage, as well as the humanlike sounds, come from a pet raccoon that went wild when it felt abandoned by the now-absent Grandpa Trenker. Buddy doesn't know about the raccoon and thinks that his grandfather must be in the bedroom. He intends to call out, "Grandfather, it's me," but surprises himself by saying "Gentlehands?" The significance of this Freudian slip showing that Buddy now accepts his grandfather's identification as the Nazi war criminal (infamously known as Gentlehands) is obscured by the emphasis on the raccoon. Readers aren't ready to concentrate on this subtle and thought-provoking climax if they are still arguing in their own minds about whether or not a raccoon could do some—but surely not all—of that damage.

Little Little

Kerr went from writing *Gentlehands,* her easiest book, to writing *Little Little,* her most difficult. She had the story in her head for a long time and over several years started and abandoned it. It was inspired by seeing the golden boy from her hometown go away to Harvard and come back with a wonderful wife. They were everyone's idea of a marvelous young couple, but then when their first child was born, she turned out to be a dwarf. Kerr stood at a distance and watched this carefree couple change into fighters for their little girl, trying to find friends for her and make her into a happy contributor to society.

As with most of Kerr's novels, she began with a real-life glimpse and then through her imagination placed herself in the situation and created a story. *Little Little* was so hard to write because she wanted some humor in it, but everything she wrote seemed dark. Also she was afraid to tell anyone that she was writing about teenage dwarfs for fear they would discourage her. One day she decided to write a newspaper essay about the story she wanted to tell but couldn't. When she was halfway through with the essay, she stopped and went back to the book, this time finishing it.

Little Little is Kerr's favorite book, not because it's the best, she says, but because it was so hard to write. "Maybe a parent who's finally raised a particularly difficult child feels this same affection and pride when that kid turns out okay."[7]

Little Little is a romance—a love story of sorts, but with a few extras. The leads are all dwarfs. They include a beautiful heiress—soon to be eighteen—and two competing suitors. Little Little is the heiress. She's extremely bright, witty, and likable. Her mother describes her as p.f. (perfectly formed), whereas one of her suitors has a hump on his back and a tooth that is out of alignment. The other suitor has a code of ethics that is somewhat askew.

The book employs alternating narrators, a device Kerr frequently uses so she can write in the first person and still get the viewpoints of both the girl and the boy. It begins with a chapter told by Sydney Cinnamon, the humpbacked dwarf. He is seventeen, and in nine pages recounts his life first at an orphanage and then as an up-state New York celebrity who makes television commercials, appears at shopping centers, and stars at openings of bowling alleys and cut-rate liquor stores. Sydney wears a cockroach costume, works for a pesticide company, and has his own theme song, "La cucaracha," as well as his own groupies: kids who gather at his appearances, waving pieces of paper for autographs.

The next chapter is by Little Little La Belle, and it opens with a rhymed invitation to Little Little's eighteenth birthday party, written by Little Little's conventional and somewhat silly mother. After the invitation, the chapter abruptly shifts style to Little Little's flip irreverence. Readers immediately see the contrast in background between Sydney's upbringing and Little Little's.

While *Little Little* is one of Kerr's funniest books, it is also one of her most serious. Its recurrent theme is people's mistrust of and sometimes cruelty to, the outsider, the odd person. Kerr cleverly offers several spoonfuls of sugar to make the story go down. For romantics, she offers the love story between Little Little and Sydney, while for cynics she offers a chaser of candid and humorous observations. And then as a further guarantee that the story will not be too harsh, she makes her heroine's problems the kinds that most teenagers would not mind having, for example deciding between two suitors and being stared at by people who smile, "the way you smile at an amusing child."

Little Little does not make friends at school because she hates going to other people's houses where everything is the wrong size. She pals around with her sister, Cowboy, and her sister's boyfriend, "who clings to Cowboy like Saran Wrap to your fingers." The one time that Little Little feels "up to" socializing is when she is driving in her own specially equipped car. Although there aren't any lines of kids in the school parking lot waiting to ride with Little Little, still she is the one extending the invitations, and she does it carefully. She invites the only black senior in school, Calpurnia Dove, who happens to be her rival in English class; "Gerald Percy, the town sissy," who has to dart past the jocks who call him "fag"; and sometimes even Dorsey Bobbin, who in the summers exposes himself to girls in Puck Park behind the rosebushes. But in Little Little's backseat "he huddles in a corner and says only, 'Here's my street,'" when they come to it.

Kerr thought Little Little's story would be appealing to teenagers because nearly all of them feel different in some way. Also, because mothers of teenagers are constantly scrutinizing their children's friends and commenting on appearances, Kerr thought that teenagers would relate to Little Little's frustration over her mother's categorization of all dwarfs as either p.f. (perfectly formed) or non p.f., as shown in Little Little's protest over her mother's criticism of Sydney Cinnamon: "If Pablo Picasso had a wart on his finger, he wouldn't be the world-famous painter in your eyes, he'd be that fellow with the wart on his finger who paints! You are all caught up in and bogged down in p.f.! Sydney Cinnamon has one of the best minds of anyone who's ever sat down at our dinner table and all you see is the tooth that sticks out!"

Authors have traditionally used visible physical characteristics as symbolic ways to communicate invisible mental characteristics; for example, Robert Louis Stevenson portrays the evil Long John Silver as maimed and ugly. A more modern and positive example is the way that Robert Lipsyte in *One Fat Summer* symbolizes Bobby's newly acquired maturity through his loss of weight. Kerr uses the physical characteristic of dwarfism as a symbolic way of talking about all feelings of differentness. It speaks well for both her skill and her sensitivity that she was able to do this in a book that is appealing to both the larger outside group of readers and to the smaller group whose physical characteristics were used as the symbol. She did not sacrifice dwarfs for the sake of her story.

Kerr has received letters from many dwarfs who have read the book and liked it (several wanting to know if it is going to be made into a movie because if so they want to try out for parts). Kerr was surprised when the mother of one dwarf told her that often p.f. dwarfs do not function sexually while deformed dwarfs do. Kerr isn't sure that she would have wanted to know this before she wrote *Little Little*.

Kerr did not attend meetings of the Little People of America nor did she interview dwarfs and their parents while writing the book. She did not want to become so close to her story that she would feel bound by actual events or restricted to writing about individuals she knew. That she succeeded in her intentions is evidenced by the accurate praise that Marilyn Kaye gave in a review. She wrote that Kerr kept the book "from becoming a shallow plea for tolerance" by putting a comfortable distance between readers and characters. Readers go away feeling that all these characters need is respect, not pity.[8]

Unlike some writers who say they do not write any differently for a teenage than for an adult audience, Kerr says that when she is writing for young people she does not assume an equivalent background of experience; she is more careful to fill in all the squares to be sure that her readers do not misinterpret what she is saying. Thus it is surely to drive home the point that *Little Little* is about differentness rather than dwarfism per se, that Kerr includes a host of characters "different" in some way: race, physical deformities, personality, emotional characteristics, occupation, etc. In fact, there are so many oddities that being different becomes the norm and some of the impact is lost. Nevertheless, Kerr should be commended for finding a new and amusing way to look at the old problem succinctly described by teenagers as being "out of it."

What I Really Think of You

What I Really Think of You is the story of two P. K.s—preachers' kids. Jesse Pegler is the son of Dr. Guy Pegler—a fancy Sunday morning television evangelist with an honorary degree from a Bible college—while Opal Ringer is the daughter of Pentecostal preacher Royal Ringer—a big, fierce-looking man whose "thick black eyebrows met at a point on his nose." His wife cautions him against pointing so much and reminds him that he has to use his nice smile once in a while or "those little tykes" that come to services at the Helping Hand Tabernacle are going to cry.

The two P.K.s happen to live in the same town, but there the similarity ends. Jesse helps his father by distributing "It's Up to You" bumper stickers to teenagers at the drive-in sunrise services and by making hospital visits where he passes out the charm of the week and tries to do the helpful little tasks that his father's manager calls "bottom-line Christianity." Jesse is usually accompanied by Seal Von Hennig, the girlfriend that his older brother Bud left behind when he ran away. Jesse doesn't know if Seal really wants to help or if she's just waiting around hoping that Bud will return. Either way, she makes herself useful. For example, while they watch Dr. Pegler's televised services she takes notes on the camera angles, the need to zoom in on more blacks and Hispanics, and those members of the choir who don't "light up" when they sing.

These aren't at all the kinds of problems that worry Preacher Royal Ringer. His biggest worry is money. (Of course, Dr. Pegler worries about money too, but on a different level.) Opal's father is concerned because his tiny flock is getting even tinier and the weekly offering is hardly enough to pay the church bills, much less support his family. He first blames his financial problems on inflation and then changes his mind: "It ain't inflation . . . it's infiltration." It's those outsiders who come right into people's living rooms on television. The competition between Jesse's and Opal's fathers seems too lopsided to be taken seriously, but then through some rather unlikely events, Dr. Pegler "steals" the Hand's "miracle." In the course of this, Jesse attends a "healing" at the Hand, and for the first time he and Opal see each other. All that Opal remembers about this first meeting is "the sickness back inside me, wanting no part of The Hand, wanting to be anyone but Opal Ringer, embarrassed for myself, the speck of my dream that doesn't know about the glow coming." Opal's mother had spoken in tongues, "danced in the spirit," and what Jesse remembers about Opal is how her white, embarrassed face with the dark eyes reminds him of the frightened little faces that his grandmother used to cut in pie crusts before she baked them. Jesse didn't know if it was his imagination or if those little pie faces really looked terrified because they knew they were going to be devoured. The other memory inspired by his first visit to the Hand is of the revival circuit and his family preaching in tents. His maternal grandfather, Reverend Jesse Cannon, "fell to his knees onstage, and cawed like a crow. . . . These sounds were sputtering out of him like blood from a fresh wound, and the eyes in his face were stark and watery like the breathless, pastel eyes of a fish at the end of a hook." Jesse had been frightened that something terrible had happened to his grandfather but his father had shushed him and whispered "He has tongues." As Jesse remembers, "once I knew he intended what he was doing up there, my bones felt as though they were melting away in the intense heat of my own humiliation. 'He's raptured.' My mother smiled down at me, and tried to take my hand, which I yanked away, wanting no part of her flesh and blood and weirdness."

Jesse doesn't tell Opal about this experience, but he is nevertheless drawn to her because of it. Still their differences are much greater than what they have in common. Jesse and his parents are invited as guests to the finest homes in Seaville. Reverend Ringer is shunned by most of the townspeople, while Opal and her mother are welcomed only when someone needs housecleaning or help with a party. Jesse drives a new car and wears designer clothes. Opal either walks or waits for her brother to pick her up in his old and undependable truck, and her best clothes are hand-me-downs that she doesn't wear for fear they will be recognized. Kerr frequently provides her readers with contrasting characters and circumstances, but the theme of contrast is seldom presented so openly as it is in *What I Really Think of You*, where the Ringers are identified as *have-nots* and the Peglers as *haves*.

Opal Ringer is a much more believable and memorable character than either Jesse or big brother Bud, perhaps because she was inspired by a real person while the Peglers are a conglomerate of all the television evangelists that Kerr has watched. Kerr says that she has long been fascinated by television preachers, especially by those such as Oral Roberts and Robert Schuller, who involve their families in their ministries. Kerr has read with interest newspaper and magazine articles about disagreements in evangelist families and has pondered over how parental pressure for a son to follow in his father's footsteps must be increased when it is begun in childhood, if not under the glare of television lights at least in front of the father's congregation. And because religion is emotion as much as it is reason, individuals are going to respond in very different ways. The family situation is further complicated by the pressure the father is under to serve as a role model, showing other parents how to keep their children in the family's religion.

Opal Ringer's part of the story came to Kerr when she was drawn into a religious store by the sounds of someone playing wonderful jazz. It was Jimmy Swaggert playing the piano. As Kerr mingled with the crowd, she saw a vulnerable looking girl standing behind the counter. Her parents owned the store. Some high school students wandered in and spoke to the girl in that mocking tone young people use when they are being cruel. Kerr was fascinated with this girl and the relationship between her and the other teenagers.

The store was affiliated with a small church that Kerr visited so she could see the girl interact with her father and mother and with those who came to services and healings. Once during a twenty-four hour revival, Kerr saw the girl standing outside.

From what she saw, Kerr said the bitterness and frustration that pentecostal preachers in small churches feel toward television preachers is very real, hence the important part Kerr gave it in her story. Kerr must have been especially touched by this girl and her family because she created an ending to Opal's story that is so wish-fulfilling for the Ringers that it loses credibility.

Bobby John Ringer, Opal's bumbling brother, had kidnapped Dr. Guy Pegler as part of a scheme to win back his girlfriend and set straight the matter of the Hand's "miracle," which Bobby John had faked. During the initial scare over the kidnapping, which brings Jesse's older brother Bud Pegler home from his self-imposed exile, Bobby John communicates with the media over his

CB radio telling everyone to be at the Helping Hand Tabernacle at ten o'clock that night, where he will bring Dr. Pegler and make his explanations.

Television crews arrive at the Hand and while everyone waits Reverend Ringer goes on with his service. The handsome Bud squeezes in to sit by Opal, looking at her in a way that gives new meaning to the choir's song, "When love shines in, how the heart is turned to singing." Opal is filled with such good feelings that to her surprise she is "slain in the spirit" and comes up singing, the way she always thought she could, but not in any language she ever heard before: "just as loud and in my own voice, soaking wet all over me, cameras going, I could see their red eyes on me, tiny red living specks, and I had tongues. I felt my body giving room to my soul while it burst into full bloom."

Several television producers invite Opal to come and sing as well as "people who have nothing to do with the Lord, and offered money," but Opal declines because she belongs to the Helping Hand Tabernacle. To hear her sing, people must come down to the Hollow. Six months later, Jesse Pegler says "She's the hottest ticket in town. They come from far and wide to see Opal, and hear her sing in tongues."

The strength of the wish fulfillment is not so much that Opal is now a star and her father's church is filled with people, but that the Ringers managed this success without compromising their principles. In contrast, the Peglers are still arguing among themselves about whether or not Jesus would have used television if it had been available. The frustrated Jesse decides that he's not going to any church for a while, a decision that his usually sensitive mother dismisses with "Oh, now *you're* going through that stage."

Instead of giving answers in *What I Really Think of You,* Kerr raises questions, which makes this one of her most provocative books. Reader's questions range from such trivial ones as "What's the 24-hour soaking that Reverend Ringer held?" to such complex ones as "How can I best decide about religion in my life?"

There are no definitive answers to many of the questions that grow out of even a casual reading of *What I Really Think of You,* but Kerr deserves credit for asking the questions in such a way that young readers will want to search for answers. It's a rare book that is as timely as Sunday morning television and that concurrently makes readers smile and contemplate both big and little questions of the inner soul.

ME ME ME ME ME

Those of us who have come to expect a new M. E. Kerr book every year look on 1983 much the way that wine lovers look on the vintage of a particularly good year. This was when Kerr published *ME ME ME ME ME—Not a Novel.*

Although it's not a novel, it's not exactly an autobiography, either. What Kerr presents are incidents or periods from her youth (early teens through her twenties). Some are written as short stories while others are more like chapters in an autobiography. As she says in an author's note, the book "is an answer to many letters from kids wanting to know if the things I write about really happened to me." If this had been Kerr's first YA book instead of her tenth there wouldn't have been any readers asking her questions nor would there have been the fascinating fictional characters for her to connect to the real life acquaintances.

The obvious assumption is that students who have read and enjoyed Kerr's previous books will be the readers for *ME ME ME ME ME,* but the reverse may also occur. Readers may happen onto it and become intrigued enough to go on to look for Kerr's novels. Kerr cleverly includes specific connections between the chapters and her other books as addendums to each section. Readers not interested or familiar with her novels can easily skip the explanations; however, few will because they have a verve and style of their own. For example, Kerr recounts going back to her hometown and having a disillusioning conversation with a man who used to be her boyfriend, the one on whom she based

Wally Witherspoon in *I'll Love You When You're More Like Me*. She concludes,

> My old pal Thomas Wolfe is wrong.
> You *can* go home again.
> You should.
> It gives you lots to think about.

As the years went by, and Kerr tried to keep from telling the same story over and over again, she created characters further and further removed from average teenagers with average problems. She began with ordinary enough Tucker and overweight Dinky Hocker, whose main problem was that she couldn't communicate with her mother. But from there she went on to create characters whose problems were more and more exotic and less and less believable. Writing stories based on her own life forced Kerr to come back from the fringes of teenage life and focus on experiences that are common to a much larger body of ordinary young people—the focus that makes *ME ME ME ME ME* so appealing.

But even in *ME ME ME ME ME* Kerr still exaggerates and bends real-life experiences to make them more interesting. For example, an amusing little joke that runs all through *Is That You, Miss Blue?* and is repeated in *ME ME ME ME ME* is the naming of school dormitories after Charles Dickens novels: *Little Dorrit, David Copperfield, Hard Times,* and *Great Expectations*. These are good fodder for Kerr's puns, but only part of the story is true. Indeed there had been an anglophile headmistress at Stuart Hall who had given British names to the dormitories, but not from Dickens. The dormitories are named Fleet, Piccadilly, High Holborn, Faith, and Upper Faith. Kerr defends taking such liberties when she explains in the prefatory author's note, "I've changed some names and details of other people involved in the incidents I describe."

The strongest and most memorable of the chapters in *ME ME ME ME ME* is chapter 3, entitled "Marijane the Spy": It's a heart-chilling story of children's cruelty to someone who is different.

The cruelty has snowballed into an avalanche too hard to stop by the time Kerr and her friends find out that the reason their new classmate, Millicent, dresses so neatly and carefully "in a little hat and gloves and shiny shoes" and that she turns "in the best compositions with the best penmanship and the straightest margins" is that she is trying so hard to look and be like anything but a convict's daughter. Millicent and her mother have come to Auburn, New York, to be near Millicent's father as he serves his term in the state prison. Kerr's statement in the afterword that "I think I felt my first real shame at how I'd treated someone, and I know that I thought of Millicent again and again as I grew up," is worth dozens of the less believable stories and didactic messages that adults are so fond of dropping on teenage ears.

The only story in the book that does not ring completely true is her account of movie-star worship in which she and a ten-year-old friend conspire to get a letter from Ronald Reagan. Marijane succeeds by telling him that she is crippled and went to see *Brother Rat* in a wheelchair.

While *ME ME ME ME ME* may never be widely popular, it will most likely have a long life span. Arthea Reed recommended the postscripts at the end of each chapter for showing "how personal experience can become the basis for a work of fiction."[9] English teachers should welcome contemporary illustrations from a writer whom young readers respect and enjoy.

ME ME ME ME ME met with generally favorable reviews. The only negative note came from people nervous that a trend might be developing in which authors, instead of creating new books for young readers, would spend their time and energy rummaging through their files for stories that didn't happen to sell or that could be reprinted and given a new life by adding a few explanatory notes about their creation. Such a criticism was probably voiced because Robert Cormier had just published *Eight Plus One,* a reprinting of nine short stories with author's explanations aimed at teenage readers, and Lois Duncan had also just published *Chapters: My Growth as a Writer.*

Nancy Hammond, writing for the *Horn Book Magazine,* compared Kerr's book to Jean Fritz's prizewinning *Homesick,* complimenting Kerr for describing "with drama, humor, and perception a youth less exotic but no less entertaining and compelling," than Fritz's, whose story was set in revolutionary China. She also complimented Kerr for being as appealing in real life as are the "smartmouth" tomboys in Kerr's novels.[10] The number of times that *ME ME ME ME ME* is either quoted or referred to throughout this volume reflects strong agreement with Hammond's positive assessment.

Him She Loves?

During the years that Kerr lived in New York City after graduating from college in 1945, she had many Jewish associates and developed a strong interest in Jewish humor and culture. She dated Jewish boys and was surprised to find herself a *goy* and to realize that to a Jewish boyfriend's mother, she did not look so good. "*Her*, he loves?" is a phrase from this period that stuck in her mind. Three decades later, she altered it to "*Him* She Loves?" which she used as the title for her eleventh YA book.

In this book, Kerr made the girl's father a Jewish comedian because she wanted the chance to have fun with Jewish humor. Also, she felt that because a Jewish comedian capitalizes on Jewish stereotypes, those stereotypes were more likely to be part of the family's life than if the father were a dentist or a teacher. Although the plot of the book is farcical, she wanted the portrayal of cultural differences to ring true.

Henry Schiller tells the story. At sixteen, he is the youngest of three brothers who with their mother have just opened a German restaurant in Kerr's fictional town of Seaville on the tip of Long Island. They have moved away from bad memories connected with their old restaurant in Yorkville, where Mr. Schiller was shot in a hold-up. Henry was twelve when his father refused to hand over $435 from the cash register, and Henry has not forgiven him for this bad decision. He would have liked to have gotten to know him. He honestly cannot remember having "had a conversation anywhere but in a kitchen, on any subject besides one like how to stuff ham horns, or roll cabbage leaves."

The story begins when Valerie Kissenwiser comes into the new restaurant to see if it will be appropriate for her sister's sweet sixteen party. As soon as she finds out that the restaurant is German, she explains that she's sorry she's made a mistake. Her grandmother is giving the party and "we're Jewish. My grandmother doesn't buy Volkswagens or Mercedes. . . ." Henry doesn't concentrate on the conversation except to understand that Valerie herself has nothing against German food, in fact she "would almost kill for good strudel," and that when Henry starts school on Monday he will probably see Valerie "around."

Henry's brothers spot his love symptoms and advise against "getting a thing" on Valerie. Henry protests, "Why do you make it sound like I'm growing a wart, or getting a fungus between my toes? I suppose you and Fred fall in love, but I get a thing."

"It's the way you go about it," Ernie answers. "You throw yourself at it like someone jumping into a fireman's net from a burning building." In spite of his brother's warnings, Henry goes right ahead and throws himself into trying to make Valerie love him as he loves her.

The main complication is that Valerie's father, nationally famous comedian Al Kiss, does not want his daughter to marry a "goy." He forbids their dating, but the restriction only heightens their longing for each other, and they devise creative ways to be together.

Al Kiss's career is not going well; his jokes are tired and he is no longer considered a fresh young talent. Then when he is on a talk show he happens to mention Valerie and his frustration that "*Him* she loves?" The audience laughs. Al Kiss has struck a sympathetic chord in the parents of America. He develops a whole new routine making fun of "Heinrich, Sauerkraut Breath." Finally, Henry begins fighting back and proves himself a worthy opponent to Al Kiss.

The book is on a grand scale, exaggerated in such a way that young readers can enjoy identifying with the characters and imagining themselves solving similar problems. Practically every sixteen-year-old boyfriend has sometimes felt that his girlfriend's parents did not think he was worthy of their daughter and has dreamed of proving differently. It's psychologically satisfying, even if not quite believable, to have such a confrontation take place on national television and to have the boy win out.

Another wish-fulfilling aspect of the story is that in the end, although Henry loses Valerie as his girlfriend, he gains Al Kiss as a substitute father. Most high school romances cannot last, but few writers of "light" fiction take their characters beyond the invitation to the prom, and it is refreshing to have Kerr show that life goes on after steadies break up.

Because of Kerr's obvious attempts to include humor through the character of Al Kiss and because of the exaggerated stereotyping of both the Kissenwiser and the Schiller families, **Him** *She Loves?* gives the impression of being almost a frothy book, written for short-term entertainment. To Jewish and non-Jewish teenagers in love with each other, family objections are indeed a serious matter. But because the issue seems to disappear in *Him She Loves?* readers do not come away pondering this issue with the same seriousness that they think about the ideas brought out in *Gentlehands, Little Little,* and *What I Really Think of You,* for example.

Kerr does not appear to have taken her usual level of care in her final revisions. Much of Al Kiss's humor is trite. This fits his character, but still it is not fun to read. There are careless slips, such as when Henry describes Valerie as wearing "a navy-blue grosgrain hairband." It is a rare teenage boy who would know what grosgrain is, much less use the word. And it is too much of a coincidence that the one time Al Kiss happens to come into Valerie's bedroom to give his daughter a fatherly talk is also the one time that Henry has come to Valerie's room and is desperately hiding behind the shower curtain in the adjoining bathroom. Coincidence becomes cliché when Mr. Kiss notices the raised toilet seat and the cowboy hat and predictably throws open the shower curtain and finds Henry.

I Stay Near You

Kerr has said that she has been hesitant to write a book set in the 1940s because as a child, she never liked to read "historical" books. Yet she is haunted by the World War II years and has long wanted to write about some of the effects on young women, whose stories have for the most part been ignored because writers were focusing on what the war did to young men. So that she could write about these years and still not seem "too" historical, Kerr used an experimental format, writing three stories about the same characters, but set in different times.

She called the resulting book *I Stay Near You* with the subtitle, "One Story in Three." A serendipitous benefit of the format, in which Kerr wrote three fairly independent stories and skipped over the events that occur between the highlighted years, is that she could introduce young readers to the cross-generational novel and still keep within the two hundred pages that most teenagers prefer for their leisure-time reading.

The book begins with "Mildred Cone in the Forties," continues with "Welcome to My Disappearance," the story of her son Vincent Haigney in the 1960s, and ends with "Something I've Never Told You," a Memorex tape that in the 1980s Mildred's grandson, Powell Storm Haigney, is making for his father, who by now has become a rock star.

Kerr is an MTV fan and welcomed the opportunity to write about popular music and musicians, something she describes as one of her "enthusiastic interests." Nevertheless, Vincent Haigney comes across as the least believable of the characters. His main function in the book is to serve as a sounding board, first for Mildred to tell her story to and then for Powell to have as the intended audience for the story he is telling on tape.

In the 1940s, Mildred lives in the west end of Cayuta near the train tracks, the dump, and the Cayuta Rope Factory. Because she wants to "better" herself, she learns to play the harp and transfers to preppy East High, where she is at best tolerated. In the summer of 1943, when the boys have gone off to be soldiers, the Cayuta Yacht Club is forced to replace bar boys with wait-resses, and so Mildred, who by now has blossomed into a buxom beauty, spends the summer carrying drinks to people out on the lawn. On a "picture-postcard afternoon" in late June, the Storms, who are owners of the Cayuta Rope Factory, dock their big boat at the club. Waitress Mildred and wealthy Powell Storm, Jr., the family's only son, have both a literal and a figurative run-in, which begins with hostility and ends with music and shining eyes. It is such an obviously special moment that everyone at the club stares, including the Storms. The narrator remembers their beautiful faces frozen in time in what turned out to be the family's last peaceful moment.

Mildred and Powell have a relatively private, but intense, love affair; Powell goes off to the war never to return; pregnant Mildred marries a tender-hearted boy with a propensity for res-cuing creatures in need. True to the genre, Mildred has a son, but does not let the Storms know.

In part 2, the boy grows almost to adulthood unaware of his relationship to the richest family in town. And true to his heri-tage, he falls passionately in love with a girl from the lower class-es—in fact from a criminal family. He is brokenhearted when she rebuffs him.

To shake her son out of his depression, Mildred tells him about his "real" father. Of course he contacts the Storms, and of course the consequences are tragic. But out of these consequences comes the narrator of part 3, Mildred's grandson, who as a high school senior tells his story through a tape being prepared as an English class assignment.

What ties all this together is a gold ring inscribed in the ma-ternal grandmother's Basque language with the message, "I stay near you." Each Storm man is to pass the ring on to his eldest son when he reaches maturity. Perhaps the bad luck begins when Powell defiantly gives the ring to Mildred because his family re-fuses to let him give her a diamond engagement ring. It continues when Mildred's son, not knowing what it is, gives it to his run-away girlfriend. The Storms reclaim it at great trouble and ex-pense, and Mildred's son in a premature farewell gesture passes it on to his own teenage son. Perhaps the luck will change now that in part 3 Mildred takes charge and for safekeeping wears the ring around her neck on a gold chain, just as she did when she was a high school girl in love with its owner.

A weakness justifiably criticized in young adult literature is its here-and-now orientation, the way it fails to relate the teen years to adult years. Because books for teenagers are relatively short, most authors focus on a single event crucial to a stage of development or a personal achievement after which the heroes walk off into adulthood much like old movie heroes fading off into the sunset. It is a strength of *I Stay Near You* that Kerr entices her readers to travel on into adulthood with Mildred Cone and to see that the threads of one's life are continuous.

Mildred's story is by far the most memorable in the book. In the beginning, she is the same kind of outsider that Kerr created in *ME ME ME ME ME* as the convict's daughter and in *What I Really Think of You* as the preacher's daughter who feels she is too good to be at the Helping Hand but not good enough to be at Seaville High. The difference in *I Stay Near You* is that readers stay with Mildred long enough to fully understand her strength and to realize that high school is not the end of the world.

Conclusion

The similarities in Kerr's dozen books are numerous. The protagonists are all bright, witty, and appealing teenagers. They have problems, but by the end of each book, the young protagonist has arrived at a new level of understanding or development. While some of the problems may be only partially solved, the endings are nevertheless upbeat. The books explore relationships among teenagers and between teenagers and adults, most often parents. And every story contains some sort of a boy/girl friendship.

Critics have told Kerr that she writes about losers. She was surprised when she first heard this, but then as she looked back at her books, she realized that yes, those characters who are the most interesting are the ones who don't have it all together yet. Kerr remembers considering herself a loner because she read so much. Even when she was in a sorority at the University of Missouri, she felt like an outsider and was convinced that her sorority was the worst one and the sorority house was just a cut-rate hotel. Now she is amused at the way she perceived her role, but she thinks her attitude is typical of most young people, who look at themselves as loners, outsiders, or losers.

Wish fulfillment plays a big part in the popularity of Kerr's books. She begins most of them with the protagonists feeling that they are losers, but within fewer than two hundred pages she turns the perception around so that those critics who say she writes about losers could as accurately say she writes about winners. The satisfying part of identifying with these characters is that they make progress through their own abilities and efforts.

Girls are excited to imagine someone falling madly in love with them as Storm Powell falls in love with poor but deserving Mildred Cone and both Jesse and Bud Pegler fall in love with the equally poor and deserving Opal Ringer. Readers can envision the glamour of learning about one's relatives through the mass media as Flanders learns about her father in *Is That You, Miss Blue?* and Buddy learns about his grandfather in *Gentlehands*.

It is intriguing to think about someone's beautiful and mysterious mother taking one's friendship as seriously as Mrs. Stein takes Alan's, to contemplate that the wealthy Suzy Slade has an ordinary after-school job not because she needs the money but because working is good, and to daydream about an eighteenth birthday party where the guests come from all over the eastern seaboard as they do to Little Little's. It is also tempting to imagine oneself eating Dinky Hocker style, which means going from restaurant to restaurant and ordering a favorite item from each menu.

But if Kerr's strength were only her ability to create wish-fulfilling situations, then her books would be little better than the hundreds of romance novels that within the last few years have begun to crowd bookstore shelves under the heading of "Young

Adult." Kerr offers considerably more than do the authors of for-
mula romance novels. The remaining pages of this book will show
what she achieves in addition to her storytelling about appealing
characters in unusual situations, and will discuss some of the
approaches she uses to keep her books from being trite and
formulaic.

What I Really Think of You

3. The Writer

Teachers, librarians, publishers, critics, and students of young adult literature may come to look back on the 1970s as a golden age in which a number of factors contributed to a landmark decade for the genre. From the economic standpoint, federal dollars were available to support public and school libraries, and children of an affluent society could afford to buy their own paperback books. But more important were changing social attitudes that gave new freedoms to authors, publishers, and readers.

Student demands for "relevance" dealt a heavy blow to the standardized lists of classics that teachers had been assigning. Such elective courses came into the high school curriculum as "Personalized Reading," "Paperback Power," and "Contemporary Reading." In these courses for average or above-average students, schools provide a large number of contemporary books from which students make their selections for individual reading followed by a conference with the teacher. The back-to-basics and the push-for-excellence movements of the 1980s caused some of these courses to be discontinued, but many teachers still include a six-week unit of individualized reading as part of more traditional courses. Also for in-class reading and discussion, they are likely to allow students to make selections from lists of contemporary books rather than to assign a whole class to read such traditional works as *Silas Marner* or *Julius Caesar*. Providing students with time and books to read is one last try by schools to instill in young people the habit of reading for pleasure.

These changes in educational practices meant that for the first time a considerable number of talented authors could support themselves by writing full-time for young readers. And professionally the work was more satisfying because of the lifting of taboos and restrictions that had always been accepted as standard for books directed at a young adult audience. When Stephen Dunning wrote his 1969 dissertation on adolescent literature, he concluded that "junior novels insistently avoid taboos . . . and are typically concerned with socially and economically fortunate families."[11] Beginning in the late 1960s, such expectations changed as shown by the successful publication of S. E. Hinton's *The Outsiders;* Paul Zindel's *The Pigman;* Vera and Bill Cleaver's *Where the Lilies Bloom;* John Donovan's *I'll Get There. It Better Be Worth the Trip;* Richard Bradford's *Red Sky at Morning;* and Ann Head's *Mr. and Mrs. Bo Jo Jones.* Like Hinton's "outsiders" or "greasers," most of the protagonists in these landmark books were far from advantaged, and the problems they met were much more serious than the will-I-get-a-date-to-the-prom variety that is what S. E. Hinton says inspired her to write *The Outsiders.* That Paul Zindel, who had won a Pulitzer Prize for his play *The Effect of Gamma Rays on Man-in-the-Moon-Marigolds,* was willing to put forth his best efforts for teenagers was tremendously important in attracting other authors, including Robert Cormier and M. E. Kerr, to the field.

In 1972, Kerr's first YA book, *Dinky Hocker Shoots Smack!,* competed for attention with Sharon Bell Mathis's *Teacup Full of Roses,* a story of a black boy whose brother was a drug addict; Lynn Hall's *Sticks and Stones* and Isabelle Holland's *The Man without a Face,* both about young men traumatized in friendships with homosexual overtones; Robb White's *Deathwatch,* a suspense thriller about a college boy battling for his life against the mad hunter that he was supposed to be guiding; Frank Herbert's *Soul Catcher,* a suspenseful story about an Indian youth battling for his heritage and his sanity; and Chaim Potok's *My Name Is Asher Lev,* about a young boy persisting against the wishes of his traditional Jewish father in his dream to become an artist.

In more ways than one, this is a formidable group of books. The authors were exceptionally skilled, their subjects new to young readers, and their approaches somber. Other notable authors publishing their first books for young adults in the 1970s were Judy Blume, Robert Cormier, Paula Fox, Rosa Guy, Virginia Hamilton, Norma Fox Mazer, and Richard Peck.

What these books have in common is the seriousness with which highly talented writers explored problems connected with sex, drugs, racial differences, physical and mental disabilities, troublesome family relationships, political problems, and feelings of worthlessness and despair. Many adults were shocked that young people responded warmly to these books, which came to be labeled "modern realism" or "problem novels." Of the successful authors, only Paul Zindel and M. E. Kerr, along with Judy Blume, who started out writing for a slightly younger audience, attempted to include humor. It was probably their humor that made them the most popular with young readers while Robert Cormier, Virginia Hamilton, and Paula Fox were more popular with adult critics. That Kerr can treat serious topics and leave her audience smiling is her biggest strength, and this talent is at the root of her initial success with *Dinky Hocker Shoots Smack!*

Considering how difficult it is for a new YA author to attract the attention of editors and thereby get reviewed (only *School Library Journal* attempts to review every book it receives), *Dinky Hocker Shoots Smack!* took a surprisingly large share of honors and attention. It was chosen to go on the 1972 best books lists compiled by *School Library Journal,* both the Children's and Young Adult Services Divisions of the American Library Association, and the Library of Congress. Subsequent books did almost as well—some better—as shown by the listing in the appendix.

The pleasure that Kerr experienced when she discovered that she could earn a living through writing young adult literature must have been considerably increased when she also discovered that she could get ample space in national review media. Being reviewed has always been important to Kerr, who early in her career made the decision to write mysteries primarily because they were the only original paperbacks that in the 1950s had a chance of being reviewed in the *New York Times*. While Kerr's mysteries would get one or two paragraphs, her YA books began to rate their own headlines. The *Horn Book Magazine,* in an unusual gesture of praise, devoted a whole page to *Is That You, Miss Blue?*, and when *Gentlehands* came out the *New York Times* published a four-column review article by Richard Bradford. In the June 1977 *Horn Book Magazine,* Mary Kingsbury published one of the first significant criticisms of Kerr as a young adult writer and concluded with:

Having published five books in four years, Kerr demonstrates the capability for sustained effort that is necessary to achieve a lasting place in literature. Time alone will determine the longevity of these novels, but it is worth noting that the last two are the best of the five. Short of writing a masterpiece, an author can establish a claim to fame by producing a number of superior books. M. E. Kerr is well on her way to that goal.

Wooing Her Readers

In her desire to receive critical notice, Kerr does not forget about her readers. She describes her goal as to:

woo young adults away from the boob tube and Pac Man not just with entertaining stories, but also with subject matter which will provoke concern and a questioning about this complicated and often unfair world we live in. I would like my readers to laugh, but also to think; to be introspective, but also to reach out . . . and I hope I can give them characters and situations which will inspire these reactions.[12]

Some authors assume that they have two or three pages in which to interest a browsing reader, but Kerr does not give herself this luxury. She took a class in headline writing for advertisers solely to help her create titles that would catch readers' eyes. She is one of the few authors whose titles are so involved that they need punctuation. She is also one of the few who asks intriguing questions such as *If I Love You, Am I Trapped Forever?* and *Is That You, Miss Blue?* Sometimes she uses a title to clarify the book's theme—as with *I Stay Near You,* which explores the ties that bind family members, and *I'll Love You When You're More*

Like Me, which shows how emotional attachments are influenced by people's expectations for the other person.

Dinky Hocker Shoots Smack! was an especially startling title in 1972 because this was when the general public first became widely alarmed over teenage drug use. The title seemed so blatantly sensational that people had to stop and take a second look to see why a respectable company like Harper and Row would be publishing such a book and why junior high librarians and teachers would be endorsing it. The turnaround in which the title accurately represents the story, but not in the way readers expect, bears resemblance to the way authors of "true confessions" stories (a trade not unknown to Kerr) attract their readers.

Kerr said she is constantly struggling with publishers to keep them from putting pictures of children on the covers of her books. Anything that makes a book look like it is intended for eleven- or twelve-year-olds, whether it is a jacket illustration, where the book is shelved in a library or bookstore, or a mention of "children's" literature, cuts down on the readership among the thirteen- to sixteen-year-olds. Kerr quite rightly observed that "No twelve-year-old minds reading a book that looks like the characters are seventeen, but no seventeen-year-old wants to read about twelve-year-olds."

Kerr designed the cover herself for the hardback edition of *Little Little* because she did not want readers to prejudge the characters based on a drawing of them. She used the title repeated in black-on-silver block letters in increasingly smaller sizes. She did not have as much influence with the paperback publishers who, she said, feel strongly that to be successful a cover must have an illustration.

Most of Kerr's fan letters are written by twelve-year-olds and have an "assignment ring" to them. Kerr ruefully observed that "Judy Blume gets the letters from kids with problems; I get the letters from kids whose teachers say they have to write an author." She wonders if the letters are truly representative of the ages of her readers or if seventh grade is the last time that teachers make this kind of assignment. (Teachers and librarians in Arizona report that Kerr's readers range from precocious ten-year-

olds up through sixteen- and seventeen-year-olds, with the ma-
jority being between thirteen and fifteen. However, older girls
read *ME ME ME ME ME* as a way of saying goodbye to Kerr and
to what they now consider childhood reading.)

The publicity and the reviews surrounding the publication of a
new book serve to keep an author's name in front of the public
and to inform potential readers about other books they may want
to read. Kerr has had the same publisher for all of her YA books
and each time a new one appears, the back of the dust jacket is
used to advertise awards that previous books have won or to
quote complimentary lines from reviews. The consistency with
which Kerr's books appear undoubtedly contributes to her popularity. But when asked if she feels pressured to write a book a
year, she says no; it is a pace that she has set for herself. She
never takes advances and so is not obligated to anyone. In answer
to the question of how long she can go on without repeating herself, she laughingly acknowledges that she constantly feels on
edge like a guest at a dinner party struggling to tell an interesting
story and being nagged by doubts: Have I already told this story
to this audience?

Kerr thinks that *Dinky Hocker Shoots Smack!* is still her most
popular book in part because it was presented as an ABC-TV Afterschool Special, even though critics were not as kind to the 1978
television production as they had been to the book. They especially criticized Mrs. Hocker, played by June Lockhart, as "over-
drawn" and "obtuse to the point of unbelievability." In the book,
Kerr had pushed Mrs. Hocker's characterization to the limits of
credibility; when the television producers were forced to reduce a
198-page book to a half-hour show, they pushed her over the line.
However, it was not the role of Mrs. Hocker, but of Nader the cat,
that bothered Kerr, who has seen the film only once, when it was
aired. (It has since been released by Learning Corporation as a
film to be shown in schools.) Kerr remembers being terribly disappointed in the cat. Nader's obesity is crucial to the plot, but the
producers cast a skinny kitten in the role. Kerr thinks they
should have used Morris, the famous Purina Cat Chow model.

The book's anti-junkfood message also caused trouble during

the television adaptation. Among the original sponsors were candy manufacturers who backed out after viewing the film, which may be one of the reasons that it was never shown as a rerun. Such complications are typical of attempts to change books into films or television productions and are among the reasons that Kerr does not see herself participating in such joint ventures. Writing a book is something an individual can do basically alone, but dramatization requires a team effort. Kerr's creativity is not the kind that can bend to the will of a team. Nevertheless, she acknowledges the potential power of the mass media in helping authors woo their readers.

A Style Appropriate to Her Subjects

Of all the literary aspects commonly discussed, the most interesting one in Kerr's books is style. When she was in high school, she was enchanted with the way Max Shulman wrote, but her English teacher confidently predicted that she would outgrow this admiration, which she did. Later on, her favorite writer was Carson McCullers. In *Love Is a Missing Person,* Miss Spring advises Suzy to read *Member of the Wedding* because "It's all about a young girl getting caught up in her brother's wedding, so caught up in it she was losing her own identity." Suzy argues that she is not having such a problem, "though sometimes I think I wouldn't mind if I was." In *ME ME ME ME ME,* Kerr writes that when she was in college she read and reread *Member of the Wedding,* finding some of her old self in Frankie, the twelve-year-old who gave herself a crewcut, changed her name to F. Jasmine Addams, and tried to go along with her brother and his bride on their honeymoon. "But more than I could see a 'yesterday me' in Frankie, I could see a future me in Carson McCullers. She became the one I most wanted to write like, and all my stories began to describe 'a green and crazy summer,' or 'a green queer dream' or 'a crazy queer green time,' on and on."

Today Kerr's style is very much her own and worth studying in its own right. Her plots, with the exception of *Gentlehands* and *Little Little,* are no more original than those in myriads of mass produced books for young people. A few of her characters are truly memorable, but when her whole cast is lined up on the stage of a reader's mind they fall into stereotypical groups simply because there are so many of them. And by restricting herself to writing about contemporary teenagers, nearly all of whom are in school, Kerr thus limits the possibilities for creating exciting and unique settings. Of course it is possible to write about a school setting in an important way, as Robert Cormier did in *The Chocolate War,* but Kerr chooses to use her settings as utilitarian, unobtrusive backdrops to her stories. The theme of nearly all YA books is that of growing up, arriving at a new stage in life. Young readers dictate the mode and tone of most YA books by refusing to read in their free time books that are somber and preachy. So like most popular writers, Kerr chooses to write in the comic and romantic modes, and she uses a humorous and irreverent tone. However, none of this detracts from the strength of her style, the way she puts details together and the care with which she struggles over phraseology and individual words.

Kerr gives an immediacy to her stories by using first-person point of view and by beginning with such atypical and therefore intriguing opening lines as:

> This story begins the winter I thought I was turning into a boy. (*The Son of Someone Famous*)
>
> Soon I would be laughed at on national television, and so in love I couldn't chew my food. . . . (*Him She Loves?*)
>
> One warm night in May, in the back of the hearse, while I was whispering "I love you. . . ." (*I'll Love You When You're More Like Me*)
>
> "Sidney," Mr. Palmer said, "you are on your way to becoming the most famous dwarf in this country. . . ." (*Little Little*)

In *What I Really Think of You,* Opal begins speaking directly to readers as though they are among the "haves" who attend Central High and make Opal feel like she's "a great, red pimple coming to a head, right in front of everyone."

If I was to say that finally Opal Ringer is going to tell you what she really thinks of you, would you laugh? You always used to laugh. I never had to do much more than just show up and you'd start nudging each other with grins starting to tip your mouths. . . .

This book illustrates how Kerr uses language to both set a mood and develop character. In keeping with her religious subject matter, Kerr surprises readers by making use of biblical language in unexpected places, such as Opal's explanation of Bobby John's failure in kidnapping Dr. Guy Pegler: "A time to be born, and a time to die, as the Bible tells it; a time to plant, and a time to pluck up that which is planted; a time to kill, and a time to heal; a time to break down . . . which is what happened to Bobby John's car that night, with Guy Pegler in it."

After Bobby John confesses to Opal that he assisted in arranging "the miracle," he and Opal drive through the countryside "with the big moon beaming down, abundance of peace, said Psalms, so long as the moon endureth." The book closes with Opal and Bud agreeing to pray for Jesse because it is something they can do together without getting into trouble. As Opal explains, "Me and him has seen the Devil's face, sweet nights when we slip, for there's the sin in us same as there's the spirit."

This is undoubtedly one of the most unusual allusions to sexual activity in all of young adult literature. Its effectiveness lies in the fact that readers are left to decide on the specifics. All they are told is that it is enough to make Opal feel guilty—which, considering her background, could be nothing more than holding hands. Then again, it could be a great deal more, considering the advice that Opal's mother gave her before her first date with Jesse:

"Satan tempts the saved more often than the unsaved honey. The unsaved's already in his camp don't you see? . . . Satan loves a setup, honey."

"Well, I'm no setup."

"I'm talking about a boy and a car, honey. That's a setup. You just remember something my own mum told me. Promise?"

"I promise."

"You must remember no one's going to buy the cow if he can get the milk free."

The homey advice that Opal's mother passes out when she tells Opal to quit looking for the holes in the doughnut or to quit tiring herself trying to get all the answers when her head and heart haven't yet learned the same language, is appropriate to Kerr's characterization of Mrs. Ringer as a woman who secretly listens to Dolly Parton, Loretta Lynn, and Crystal Gale, "and would any day rather hear Loretta sing 'It wasn't God Who Made Honky Tonk Angels' than a whole heavenly choir sing 'Abide with Me.'"

Kerr is skilled at observing and compactly presenting details that tell a world about a character, such as her comments that Little Little will "never stand taller on two legs than the family dog does on four," that Suzy Slade in *Love Is a Missing Person* could not face deep subjects with her mother because their "own relationship was too shallow," and that Suzy's father gave his new wife a diamond "about the size of a Midol tablet." At other times Kerr's characters circle around the meanings of words, as when Miss Spring's baby-faced soldier signs his photo, "For Gwen, my love, all ways, always." Giggling Nan explains to Suzy that it is "the big D. M."—the double meaning.

Dialogue as a Revelation of Character

Although Kerr has said that she is not interested in writing movie or television scripts, she would be very good at it because she is a master at creating dialogue. She gives her sharpest lines to her characters in dialogue, as in *What I Really Think of You* when Jesse Pegler accuses Seal Von Hennig of being a P.K. group-ie. Kerr is being more than amusing here. She is letting Jesse accuse his family of being in show business rather than religion since actors and singers are usually the ones with "groupies."

Thumbing through any of her books, one seldom sees a page of type uninterrupted by quotation marks. Some pages look almost like a script, as does the scene from *Him She Loves?* where Henry sneaks away from his restaurant work to telephone Valerie. It is Valentine's night, and her father has just appeared on a late night talk show where he got big laughs talking about Henry as a mental case with sauerkraut breath. Valerie's grandmother, Mrs. Trump, is usually the one who answers the telephone at the Kissenwiser home:

> The phone rang once, twice.
> "You forgot Mom's orchid, too," Ernie [Henry's older brother] said.
> "Mom hasn't gone on yet. They were playing 'Schnitzelbank.' Didn't you hear everyone singing?"
> "Mom's going on any minute," Ernie said.
> Mrs. Trump said, "Hello?"
> "I'd like to talk to Valerie, please."
> "From The Restaurant?" Mrs. Trump said. "Is that you?"
> "From The Restaurant. Heinrich. Mental Case. Sauerkraut Breath. Yes. It's me. I'd like to talk to Valerie, please, Mrs. Trump."
> "Hoo-ha! You got some nerve saying what you'd like at forty-five minutes before midnight and she's got school tomorrow."
> "I've got school tomorrow, too."
> "Talk at school, not in the middle of the night. We go to bed around here."
> "Mrs. Trump," I said, "I know you just watched him on TV. I know you're not asleep."
> "You're putting me to sleep." She actually snored into the mouthpiece. "There. I'm asleep."
> Click.
> "Henry, the apple pancakes need their coffee! *Now!*"

This conversation, typical of dozens of others, illustrates how Kerr juggles several balls at the same time. First, the interruptions from big brother Ernie give readers the feeling of being in a noisy restaurant kitchen where they, along with Henry, are forced to divide their attention. The information that the band is playing "Schnitzelbank" and that everyone is singing adds to the noise level as well as reminding readers that this is a German restaurant where "the apple pancakes need their coffee! *Now!*" Readers have met Grandmother Trump on the telephone before so they recognize her "Hoo-ha!" and her abrupt and questioning manner. But still it is impressive how consistently Kerr distinguishes the speaking styles of even minor characters. A less skilled writer would be forced to clutter up such dialogues with "Mrs. Trump said," "Henry responded," and "Ernie shouted," etc.

Kerr's ability to zero in on characteristic details of people's speech allows her to establish their backgrounds without intruding herself into the fast-moving plots. In *Love Is a Missing Person*, Suzy's father falls in love with a cocktail waitress who pronounces Oedipus "oh-ead-a-puss." In *What I Really Think of You*, Bobby John, who is thanked for bringing a crippled girl into the Hand for healing, says modestly, "Well, I was her mintor all right." Reverend Ringer scoffs at his son's mistake saying that he sounds as if he were in charge of her breath. In *Is That You, Miss Blue?*, Flanders's Grandmother Brown gives as the reason for Flanders's mother running away to establish her own life in New York City, "Many women can't resist Italian [which she pronounces 'eyetalian'] men. I've seen it in the movies."

It must have been a jolt for Flanders to leave the gracious southern speech patterns that surrounded her at Charles School and to arrive at her mother's New York apartment house and be greeted by the building superintendent:

"I don't know no Ruth Brown."

"Ruth Deacon?"

"Miss Deacon? Yea, but she ain't got no daughter your age. She ain't got no daughter, period, that I know about."

"Why would I lie?"

"Why do pigs whistle, miss? Don't waste my time. Miss Deacon's at work."

"Where?"

"You're her daughter but you don't know where she works? Cute."

"I am her daughter," I said.

"I'm her nephew, miss; I'm her great-grandpa. But I don't go inside her apartment when she ain't home."

"Can I wait here in the lobby?"

"Free country." He ducked back inside his apartment and shut the door.

A more subtle technique of Kerr's is changing the speech patterns of her characters as an indication of growth. P. John Knight in *Dinky Hocker Shoots Smack!* comes into the story with a chip on his shoulder. Readers first meet him in a creative writing class where he reads his poem "Thanks to the United Nations."

> Aren't you glad the Chinese are in the U. N. now?
> Oh boy? And how!
> Who wants to live forever?
> Do you? Do I? Welcome, slant-eye. . . .

When the teacher observes that his thirteen lines are more politics than poetry, P. John responds with

"All great poets mix politics with poetry: Yevtushenko, Joel Oppenheimer, Pablo Neruda."
"Who's Pablo Neruda?" Mr. Baird asked.
P. John heaved an exasperated sigh. "He *only* won the Nobel Prize for 1971, Professor!"

P. John continues in this manner all through the winter, finally leaving Brooklyn Heights and going away to an experimental school. When he comes back for a surprise visit to Dinky, it is Dinky who has the chip on her shoulder. When she refuses to apologize as her mother demands, P. John's new maturity is obvious in his simple statement, "Let her go. I don't think she needs a surprise like this."

Natalia Line, Dinky's cousin, changes her speech patterns depending on how psychologically comfortable she feels. When she's nervous or upset she speaks in rhyme. In other books, characters do it just for fun: in *ME ME ME ME ME*, Marijane the Spy and her friends have a rhyming dialogue they use to tease the new girl in town about her mother's job: "You know, a hick doesn't take the tickets like a city slicker does. You have to be very, very quicket to take a ticket." In *Gentlehands*, as Buddy Boyle is going off to read his Grandfather's farewell message, his boss lightens the somber moment by admitting that he plans to escape life's harsh realities: "Grass will put you on your ass and make time pass." When Buddy and Skye smoke the marijuana that Buddy took out

of the wastebasket at the Sweet Mouth, Kerr uses a rhyming dialogue to communicate their pleasurable and sexy feelings:

> "Whoosh-dang the bore is shut," I said.
> "Are you the bore?"
> "I'm glut," she said. "I'm hungry."
> "I'm butt," I said. "Sit on me."
> "I'm slut," she said. "I run around a lot."
> "I'm Tut," I said. "I'm a king."
> "I'm rut," she said, "and you're in me."
> "I'm cut," I said, "and I'm open."
> "I'm mutt," she said. "Bowwow."

These lines sound more forced than most of Kerr's rhymes, but
they do prepare readers for the tender love scene that follows.

Fresh Metaphors

Kerr uses metaphors both to create vivid pictures and to develop characterization. Sabra St. Amour's stage mother reveals her
brassy, New York personality when she tells Sabra, "You're not
just another salami decorating the deli ceiling—you're special."
To Fedora, the director of Sabra's show, who comes to the beach
house and begins to hint coyly at new plans, Madame St. Amour
says, "I wish you'd pee or get off the pot, because the suspense is
killing yours truly." Kerr writes that Fedora winced at the vul-
garity, which tells readers something about Fedora and at the
same time protects Kerr from those who might criticize her for
writing such slang: she has at least acknowledged its
inappropriateness.

Many of Kerr's metaphors are used for surpise or comic relief.
In the fairly somber *Is That You, Miss Blue?* one of the students
at Charles School is the daughter of a newly affluent Appalachian
coal miner. When the father comes to visit in his white monogrammed Cadillac, Flanders goes with the girl's family to have
dinner at the town's fanciest hotel. As they cross the lobby, a cous-

in tells Flanders that her eyes are going to pop right out of her head if she orders a steak because "they come big as toilet seats!" Back at school, a teacher advises Flanders to break off her friendship with Carolyn Cardmaker because "If you walk with ducks, you start waddling before long." These metaphors bring funny pictures to mind which amuse readers and allow them to return to the story feeling refreshed.

The appeal of Kerr's comparisons is their basis in everyday material familiar to teenagers. For example, Opal Ringer prepares readers to understand her brother's frustration by observing that he was "supposed to be following in Daddy's footsteps, but it was like an ant trying to put his legs down in elephant tracks." His sermons "got worse as he went along. His nerve ran out on him, like a cat running from the fleas on her own back." Opal shows how estranged she feels from the other teenagers by stating, "You never changed me, just made me dig deeper under my strangeness, made me pull the crazy blanket over my head to look out at your real world through eye slits."

In *I'll Love You When You're More Like Me,* Wally Witherspoon is unofficially engaged to Harriet Hren, but Lauralei Rabinowitz keeps returning to his thoughts "like mildew you can't get off a suitcase no matter how often you set it out in the sun." He has fallen in love with Lauralei "the way a storm rages, or a rock number builds, the way you fly in dreams all by yourself, or go down a roller coaster smiling while you're screaming."

Foreshadowing

Another of Kerr's strengths is the foreshadowing with which she prepares her readers, so that even though they may not know exactly what is going to happen, they have a sense of satisfaction at the end—a feeling that things worked out as they should have. For example, early in *Gentlehands* readers are warned that things are not always as they appear when Skye and Grandpa Trenker are talking about birds. Skye says, "I really admire birds, they're so *free*. I mean they *symbolize* freedom." Trenker explains that this is a false notion because birds cannot move from one area to another. They are very restricted, "prisoners, really, of their own territory." Trenker's description could as easily have been of himself as of the birds. Although to Skye and Buddy he appears to have everything, he is very much a prisoner of his past. His freedom of movement is so limited that at the end of the book when he is forced to change locations, he ironically describes himself as a package being sent somewhere. A second warning about things not being what they appear is contained in a lesson Trenker gives Buddy in self-confidence: "You can become anything you want to be," he tells Buddy. "It's a matter of authority. Whatever a man's confidence, that's his capacity." That Trenker sincerely believes this and has apparently had experiences that taught it to him, prepares readers to accept the conclusion of the book.

Early in *Him She Loves?,* the fate of Valerie's and Henry's relationship is foreshadowed. Kerr shows the temporary nature of young romances when Henry's first-day conversation with Valerie is interrupted by a phone call from his previous girlfriend. She is remembering last New Year's Eve and wants to know if he is remembering too. When he begins telling her about Valerie Kissenwiser and her famous father, she says, "I'm glad I called because now I know for once and for all it's over." Henry's response is that it was finished a year ago at Christmas, "one-hundred-and-sixty-five dollars for a ring she tossed out the window of a taxi. That's over."

Henry had bought his girlfriend a ring for a Christmas present, but he had spoiled the romance of the moment by accompanying the gift with an explicit statement that in no way was it to be considered an engagement ring. The girlfriend had responded with the kind of grand gesture that most women dream about but cannot bring themselves to make. She threw it out the window.

Even before the telephone call, readers know that Henry's thoughts are now on Valerie Kissenwiser because he purposely let her leave her cashmere gloves at the restaurant and made note of what she said about loving strudel. In the time he has before the dinner hour he decides to return Valerie's gloves to her, along with a carefully wrapped strudel. He calls on the telephone, and when her grandmother answers and says, "Henry *who?*," he forgives her telephone manners with the significant statement, "That's all right. You don't know me yet." A few moments later, with the help of a road map, Henry begins his journey through a blinding snowstorm to the heart of Valerie Kissenwiser.

In *ME ME ME ME ME,* alert readers will guess that the child Marijane and her friends tease mercilessly is different because she is a convict's daughter. Early in the story, Kerr tells how Marijane hates to go to the dentist in Syracuse but loves to ride the bus because she would often get to see state prisoners on it. If they had just been released, they might have a birdcage with them since the men were allowed to have birds as pets. But if they were coming in they would be slouched in their seats, maybe handcuffed to other men, but still looking out at their last glimpses of freedom.

This description is ostensibly made to explain why "young girls, alone, weren't often on the bus," and hence why Marijane's attention was drawn to Millicent. The real purpose of the statement, however, is to prepare readers for the climax of the story, which reveals that the brightest, most conscientious and self-conscious seventh grader in the school is living in Auburn to be near her imprisoned father.

Even the title of *If I Love You, Am I Trapped Forever?* lightly foreshadows the end of Leah and Alan's romance. A stronger element of foreshadowing lies in Alan's words:

> Whenever I feel great, I think something's going to happen as punishment. I'll go blind or deaf or wake up from the dream. That afternoon I decided my punishment would be that I'd flunk Latin and not graduate with my class. I made a dive for my book bag.
> That was when I found it.

What he found was a letter from Duncan to Leah, which indeed foreshadowed the end of their going steady.

Another incident is foreshadowed when Alan tells Mrs. Stein how mature he has become: "I don't even remember the past anymore." She smiles and wistfully advises him that those who don't remember the past are condemned to relive it. These words jump back into the reader's mind when Mrs. Stein runs away with the alcoholic football coach. She apparently plans to rescue him from his alcoholism just as she had rescued Mr. Stein a decade earlier.

Kerr's Light Touch

The compliment young readers are most likely to give Kerr is that she is a funny writer. Scholars have yet to agree on a definition of *humor*, but they do agree that humor contains some kind of a surprise or incongruity. Kerr digs out life's little incongruities, exaggerates them to the point of ridiculousness, and then sprinkles them through her books, where they serve various purposes.

The incongruity of mixing humor and religion is a recurring element in *Is That You, Miss Blue?* Mr. Diblee tells a joke about an Episcopalian minister who was often mistaken for a Catholic priest. The punch line is "He's no Father, he's got four kids!" After Miss Blue puts the crucifixion painting in the bathroom, the girls make fun of her by devising such nicknames as "O torn cheeks," "Thorn-brain," and "O fingers-nailed."

Later, Kerr uses humor as a double-edged way of revealing character. Cardmaker's description of "The Rich" in such places as "their drawing room," "their library," "their Rolls Royce" or "on their way to the stock market," "on their way to a huge costume ball overlooking a canal in Venice," and "just coming back from safari" reveals as much about Cardmaker as it does about "The Rich." The same is true of Cardmaker's sarcasm about some of the other students: she says that "For Sue Crockett, hell will be a place where no one knows her mother drives a Mercedes," and "For Ditty Hutt, heaven will be a place where you can marry your own brother," while for Miss Balfour "hell will be a place with no mirrors."

Many of Kerr's jokes do nothing more than bring a quiet smile, as in *Dinky Hocker Shoots Smack!* when Tucker expects to be chewed out by P. John "for suckering him into a date" with overweight Dinky, but all that P. John says is "Susan's got a mind like a steel trap. She's okay!" Tucker is surprised because he "had never given any thought to Dinky's mind. It was not the main thing the average person meeting Dinky noticed."

Other times the humor points out such ironies as the tyranny of dieting, a terrible punishment that people decide to inflict on themselves. Dinky tells Tucker that P. John is a Jean Nidetch fascist, someone who doesn't care about the individual, but only "about a cause—like Weight Watchers." When Tucker asks "Who's Jean Nidetch?" Dinky replies, "The Weight Watchers' dictator. She dresses all in white and carries one red rose."

After the awards ceremony when a very upset Mrs. Hocker and a very angry Mr. Hocker are looking for Dinky, Tucker feels sorry for Natalia, who has to stay home and hide Dinky as well as fend off Mrs. Hocker's rage. But then Mr. Hocker says to Tucker: "You come along to the deli with me," and suddenly Tucker feels sorry for himself. Readers, who have been in similar situations, smile with relief that it is Tucker and not them who is suddenly pulled into some other family's argument.

Both teenagers and adults are interested in the bizarre and the weird—witness the popularity of tabloid newspapers. Kerr capitalizes on this fascination with Dinky Hocker sharing such stories as the one about the man with the wooden arm and the hook who would bang on the windshields of young lovers' cars and try to get in the cars to steal the girls away. Dinky swears that a girl who went to St. Marie's had been up in Prospect Park with her boyfriend. They started talking about the man and grew so frightened that they drove away. The boy took the girl home and then went to his own house. When he opened his door, he found a hook from a wooden arm caught in the door handle. As Dinky explains, "They must have driven off just as he was about to open the door."

The Power of Kerr's Names

When it comes to creating names, Kerr resembles a character in *Little Little* who is fittingly called Opportunity Knox because he constantly schemes to get something extra for himself. In a similar way, Kerr schemes to get extra mileage out of a limited number of words by making almost every name she creates do double duty.

Like a poet, she manipulates sounds, relying on such devices as repetition, alliteration, and rhyme as in the names Little Little, Belle La Belle, Carolyn Cardmaker, Wallace Witherspoon, Dirtie Dotti, Buddy Boyle, Sabra St. Amour, Gloria Gilman (nicknamed Gee Gee), $uzy $lade, and Miss Grand from Videoland. These poetic names serve as an amusing memory aid to readers, an important function in books that may have as many as twenty characters.

Kerr also creates names from sets of words that readers are already accustomed to hearing together. Saint Vincent, the rock star in *I Stay Near You,* has a name with a familiar ring to it because he is named after Edna St. Vincent Millay, his parents' favorite poet. The name is not only easy to remember, but reminds readers of an important part of the plot. Similarly, Opal Ringer's name reminds readers that she is a have-not rather than a have, like an opal ring compared to a diamond.

Many times Kerr will choose a name apparently just for the sound of it, but later she will return to use it in a pun. For example, Sydney Cinnamon is a catchy, alliterative name for the dwarf hero of *Little Little,* but Kerr makes more of it than that. When Andrea Applebaum's mother hires him to be BABY 1979 at a New Year's Eve party, he and Andrea grow romantic in the basement and Andrea croons, "Cinnamon and Applebaum. Put us together and we're a pie."

Early in *Little Little,* Kerr uses names not only to introduce the Twin Orphans' Home where Sydney grew up, but also to amuse readers and to establish a flip, offbeat tone. Sydney, who is narrating the story, explains that he lives in Miss Lake's—commonly called Mistakes—cottage. His cottage mates include legless Wheels Potter, who gets around on a board with roller skates attached; Bighead Langhorn, who has a short, skinny body but a head the size of an enormous pumpkin; Cloud, a one-armed albino with a "massive head of curly white hair"; and Pill Suchanek, whose mother took some kind of drug before she was born that left Pill with flippers for arms. The teacher is named Robert but nicknamed Robot because "his only facial expression was a smile, his only mood cheerful." Of course Miss Lake disapproves of this dark humor and scolds, "Don't call Albert 'Cloud.' . . . His name is Albert Werman." Cloud insists that he likes the name because before he came to Twin Oaks he was "Albert Worm, or just plain Wormy," a nickname that reappears in *I Stay Near You.*

Typical of the group's wordplay and attitude is the nickname Sara Lee, which they use to refer to all those who do not live in Miss Lake's cottage. The name is an acronym for Similar And Regular And Like Everyone Else, a succinct expression of a theme that Kerr had already explored in *I'll Love You When You're More Like Me.* Kerr names her society for dwarfs The American Diminutives or TADpoles. She calls the organization for the parents PODS, for Parents of Diminutives. Larry La Belle refers to Little Little's contrasting suitors as Mr. Clean (also known as Mr. White Suit) and The Roach. Little Little's sister is called Cowboy, because she was "supposed to have been the long-awaited boy, Larry La Belle, Jr.," and she started riding horses before her feet could even reach the stirrups. Cowboy's boyfriend is the teenage son of a Japanese entrepreneur. He is nicknamed Mock Hiroyuki, which looks and sounds right for a Japanese name, but there's nevertheless something amusing about it. Is he a mock boyfriend? He doesn't act much like a real one. Or perhaps because he is in the process of becoming Americanized, he is now only mock Japanese (c.f. mock turtle soup or mock cheese cake). Or perhaps he's a mock hero or a yucky hero.

Even in the autobiographical *ME ME ME ME ME,* Kerr plays with names, but because of the disclaimer in the preface, "I've changed some names and details of other people involved," it is hard to know which bits of name play are taken from memory and which are the result of the linguistic skill that Kerr has developed in a lifetime of writing. I suspect that most instances are the latter. From the journal her father kept, she quotes, "Our daughter is dating the local undertaker's son, Donald Dare, tall, dark, and harmless. Dares very little is my guess." This wonderful two-liner sounds too smooth to have been written in a daily journal. Marijane's father probably expressed a similar thought, but it was left to the writer, M. E. Kerr, to make up the alliterative name Donald Dare, which, in addition to the possible pun, is amusing because it sounds like Donald Duck.

In *Dinky Hocker Shoots Smack!* readers learn right away that Tucker's uncle is a "ding-a-ling." His "name was Guy Bell, but everyone called him Jingle, and he was not the type who minded." On the day before Dinky starts a new diet, she buys herself two chocolate-dip ice cream cones and to her mother's horror explains to Tucker that she is gorging before she gets injected with a hormone made from pregnant women's urine. Each injection will cost five dollars and Dinky will get one shot a day. The hormone is amusingly named Follutin—*fallopian* as in *tube* and *falutin* as in *high*.

When Dinky is feeling sorry for herself, she confides to the cat, "Dinky Dull and Nader Nowhere—that's us all right." When Dinky's liberal father wants to deride the beliefs of Dinky's conservative friend, P. John, he calls him Eric Establishment. It is significant to the plot that P. John is the only one who calls Dinky by her given name, Susan. Near the end of the book, Tucker, without giving the matter any thought, also begins calling her Susan, and P. John says "Thanks for finally calling her Susan." By drawing attention to this, Kerr prepares for the climax, Tucker's conversation with Dinky's father after the ordeal of the awards ceremony and the discovery of the graffiti. As Mr. Hocker's anger winds down, he looks at Tucker and asks, "And Susan's safely home?" "Tucker nodded and smiled slightly . . . not at Mr. Hocker, exactly; more at the soft sound, 'Susan.'" This is the clue that lets readers know Dinky is going to make it.

In *I'll Love You When You're More Like Me,* Sabra St. Amour tells how her mother used to come bursting into her room, turn off Elvis and say, "What are we doing lollygagging around here like Mrs. Average and her daughter, Mediocre? Let's go to the Apple for some fun!" As Sabra explains, this was back in the "Dark Ages when Sam, Sam Superman" had them trapped in suburbia and Sabra's name was Maggie. Now that she is a big star, she and her mother can laugh at the old days, which are as different from their glamorous new life as the name Maggie Duggy is from Sabra St. Amour.

Kerr uses a similar incident in *If I Love You, Am I Trapped Forever?* It is not the protagonist, however, who finally gets the right name; it is his nemesis, the boy he nicknamed Doomed. Alan is amazed when he hears his girlfriend, Leah, refer to Doomed as Duncan. When he expresses surprise, Leah says, "Alan you couldn't believe I *care* anything about Dunc!" As Alan observes, "From Doomed to Duncan to Dunc was a long distance in a very short space of time."

In *Gentlehands,* Kerr openly acknowledges the importance she places on names. She uses Skye Pennington's high-sounding name (high as the sky and penthouse) as the narrative hook to get readers interested in a romance between the boy who is telling the story and a girl who is out of his social class. The book begins with Buddy wondering what the summer would have been like if he had never met Skye Pennington. He muses: "They always seem to have names like that, don't they? Rich, beautiful girls are never named Elsie Pip or Mary Smith. They have these special names and they say them in their particular tones and accents, and my mother was right, I was in over my head or out of my depth, or however she put it."

The title of the book *Gentlehands* comes from the ironic name given to one of the most cruel Nazi SS guards at Auschwitz. The guard would taunt his Jewish prisoners from Rome by playing Puccini's opera *Tosca* and singing "O dolci mani," which translates "gentle hands." The boy in the book has the plain name of Buddy Boyle, and his family is among those who refer to the Hadefield Country Club as the Hate-Filled Club, a pun that Kerr used earlier in *Love Is a Missing Person* to communicate the resentment that exists between ordinary townspeople and wealthy owners of seaside estates such as the Pennington's five acres named Beau-regard. Buddy's father disgustedly refers to Skye as Miss Gott-bucks from Beaublahblah. Even the names of the characters' pets give telltale evidence of social class. The Penningtons own Pap-illon (*butterfly* in French) dogs named Janice, January, and Little Ophelia. Buddy does not own a dog, but his upper-class grand-father has a keeshond named Mignon. Trenker says the name is taken from the opera, but a more gruesome interpretation is that it comes from *filet mignon,* a reminder of how Trenker used to turn selected prisoners over to his dogs.

When Skye introduces Buddy to her friends, he is surprised to meet a boy named "Connie as in Conrad." In Buddy's crowd, any boy with such a name would not have gone by this nickname. Toward the end of the book, Kerr gets double use out of the name Connie in a way that again highlights the differences in Skye's and Buddy's backgrounds. Skye tells Buddy that "Connie Sprec-kles has a new Connie." Buddy does not understand and so Skye explains, "A new Lincoln Continental." Buddy feels condescended to when Skye adds, "Everybody calls them Connies." This conver-sation takes less than half a page, but it is enough to let readers know that the leaves are beginning to fall on this summer romance.

Kerr again uses an incident with names to advance the plot when Buddy's grandfather tells his social-climbing grandson that he needs "a man's name." Buddy can't use his first name because then he would be confused with his father, and so he decides to use his middle name, Raymond. He tells his best friend, Ollie, that he wants to be called Ray. Ollie at first feigns approval, but then as he announces that instead of being called Ollie he wants to be called Gertrude, he "raised his pant leg, flung his ankle back, and howled." This incident shows how naively Buddy ac-cepts whatever his grandfather says and hints to readers that perhaps Buddy should follow Ollie's example and be a bit more skeptical.

In *Is That You, Miss Blue?,* Cardmaker is a card, but the name earns no special comment. However, an explanation of her roommate's name is worked into the story as a way of indicating differences in the backgrounds of most of the girls at the school who come from "old" families and occasional girls from newly affluent "hillbilly" families. The roommate's name is Cute Dibblee, "and Cute isn't a nickname either. She's got a sister called Sweet."

As a light touch in a fairly serious book, the girls call the headmistress APE because she signs disciplinary notes with her initials, Anna P. Ettinger. The school's secret honorary society was named the ELA. The initials stood for nothing more exciting than the Episcopal Library Association, but the girls who were not invited to join took out their resentment by saying the initials stood for Extra Lucky Asses.

The name Ernestine Blue is appropriate for the religious teacher, Miss Blue, because blue is a sacred color often associated with the Virgin Mary. The fact that the story's protagonist also has a color name, Flanders Brown, shows that the two have something in common, foreshadowing their special student/teacher relationship.

Kerr's awareness that it takes only a tiny change to bring about a very different connotation is illustrated by one of the other teachers telling Flanders that she had gone to school with Ernestine Blue, who had been called Nesty and was chased by all the boys. In another reversal on a name, Miss Blue teaches her chemistry class about snob gases, those "that refuse to combine with anything else under any conditions." Miss Blue explains that while their discoverer, Cavendish, had named such things as argon and neon "noble gases because of their elite quality, she preferred to think of them as the snobs."

It's a similar kind of incongruity that in *Love Is a Missing Person* makes Suzy and Nan laugh hysterically when they see Gwendolyn Spring's nameplate and realize how close but yet how far apart are "Miss G. Spring" and "Miss G. String". In *The Son of Someone Famous*, the students say about their teacher Ella Early that she is "Ella Late who has no fate," and in *Him She Loves?*, it is amusing when the fattest boy in the social problems class is assigned to play the role of an anorexic called Anna Rexy and when the biggest midyear social event is the Dead of Winter Dance. Although people are to come as someone dead, the music will be "LIVE from Ironing Bored."

Alert readers can find many other examples of interesting names in Kerr's books. She uses them to help her readers remember her characters' names and personalities and the roles they play. Sometimes she uses a name to hint at things too bizarre to say or to establish a particular tone or move the plot along. But mostly she looks on naming as an opportunity for both author and reader to have fun. She is so accustomed to getting double meanings out of the names she creates, that she now does it almost subconsciously and sometimes surprises herself. For example, she said it was only after she turned in the manuscript for *ME ME ME ME ME* that she made the connection between the word *me* and the initials of M. E. Kerr.

Conclusion

One of the speculations about the reason that Laura Ingalls Wilder was able to remember so many details from her pioneer childhood and write about them with such clarity in the *Little House* books is that as a child she was constantly describing her physical surroundings and whatever was happening for the benefit of her blind sister. This made Laura a careful observer and gave her practice in accurately describing places and events. There may be a similar explanation of why Kerr is so good at remembering the emotional highs and lows of teenagers. Although she never described her surroundings for a blind sister, she was constantly describing actions and emotions through the stories she began writing while she was in high school. Besides helping her develop writing skills, the act of putting her thoughts and experiences on paper may be one of the reasons that Kerr can keep going back to the well and coming up with fresh ways to tell about the hilarity and agonies of being young.

To get her story ideas, Kerr watches people—but always from a distance. She does not want to get so close that she would miss the fun of seeing what her own psyche will do with someone else's situation. "Writing a book," she has said, "is like going on a trip. You just hope that at the beginning you don't choose companions who will bore you before you get to the end."

I'll Love You When You're More Like Me

4. The Teacher

Just as do most adults who work with young people, Kerr wants to pass on the wisdom of the world to succeeding generations. Teaching through fiction got a bad name from the moralistic tracts that previous generations pressed upon helpless children, but Kerr does not indulge in that kind of didacticism. Instead she breezes into teenagers' lives like an Auntie Mame—more experienced and worldly than their friends and less uptight and protective than their parents. Young readers are flattered because she treats them as though they are respected party guests worthy of her best efforts at charm and wit.

Kerr's books abound with mentors, usually a teacher, librarian, or employer, but sometimes just a stranger who happens onto the scene. For example, the druggist in *The Son of Someone Famous* takes it upon himself to scold Adam Blessing for listening in on Brenda Belle's request for a depilatory: "'What's the matter with a boy like you?' he said. 'A boy like you ought to use his head. That was a highly personal transaction. A gentleman steps aside in such a circumstance, in case you didn't know.'"

When Alan in *If I Love You, Am I Trapped Forever?* goes to New York to meet his father, he is appalled at the bickering between his father and stepmother. The stepmother sees his reaction and tries to explain that husbands and wives sometimes get to know each other so well and grow so accustomed to each other's moods that they dispense with ordinary civilities. "It probably isn't right, but it isn't as wrong as it seems to an outsider, either."

The more typical mentor is someone with a long-term relationship such as Little Little's teacher, Miss Grossman, or Suzy

Slade's boss at the library, Miss Gwendolyn Spring. The observations that Miss Spring shares with Suzy range from "Amicable divorces are always easier when there's a lot of money," to "It's too bad such a compelling love wasn't directed my way. But that would have made things even and fair and not at all like life."

Occasionally the mentoring role is played by a contemporary. Suzy's sister tells her: "You're like some little kid who's afraid to step out of the house until she knows exactly what's going on, and if she'll be absolutely safe. My advice is to get your ass out the door and take your chances like everyone else. You're not five years old anymore!"

For the most part, Kerr's characters share their observations in such a natural way that readers do not feel that someone is trying to teach them something, even when in *Little Little* Sydney Cinammon shares a whole bibliography of books about "different" people. He explains that at Mistakes, "Cloud never read books about normals. He said there was always a ring of untruth in them." The books that got passed around, the ones that were dogeared and covered with fingermarks, included *Very Special People* by Frederick Drimmer, *Freaks* by Leslie Fiedler, *The Dwarf* by Par Lagerkvist, *Leo and Theodore* and *The Drunks* by Donald Newlove, *Freaks Amore* by Tom De Haven, *The Geeks* by Craig Nova, *Memoirs of a Midget* by Walter de la Mare, and *The Elephant Man* by Ashley Montagu. Of course, "all such books were frowned on by Miss Lake."

As far back as Little Little can remember, her grandfather has been working to help her develop a positive attitude toward her dwarfism. He isn't always successful. For example, she does not like the poem he used to whisper in her ear, "If you can't be a pine on top of the hill," you should be "the best little scrub by the side of the rill." Little Little definitely does not want to be a scrub bush, not even the best little bush on the side of a hill. But she likes her grandfather to tell about famous and successful people who were dwarves: artist Toulouse-Lautrec, miniaturist Richard Gibson, the powerful Attila the Hun, a spy in the French Revolution named Richebourg, and the king of Lydia in Asia Minor, from whom we get the phrase "rich as Croesus."

Grandfather La Belle speaks disdainfully about Tom Thumb because rather than using his brains he allowed himself to be exploited.

"What does 'exploit' mean, Grandfather?"
"It means to utilize for profit. This Barnum fellow made a lot of money satisfying the public's curiosity about what someone different looks like. He turned Tom Thumb into a sideshow! . . . That's no way to live your life, Little Little, and he's no example to follow!"

Sometimes Kerr's characters act as their own mentors, figuring things out and sharing their thoughts. In *Is That You, Miss Blue?* Flanders gets a note from Sumner Thomas. He is the boy who is going to take her to the upcoming dance, and his note reads "Don't ever change." Since they've never seen each other, she finds this an especially strange message and decides there must be something mentally wrong with him. Worrying about the upcoming date gets her so upset that she experiences what her pop psychologist father calls "severe angst." She treats herself by remembering one of the exercises he teaches his clients at Attitudes, Inc. It consists of stretching out with your feet raised above your head, then shutting your eyes and remembering a difficult time from which you thought you'd never recover, then figuring out how you recovered and why. Realizing that you succeeded before is supposed to give you the encouragement needed to do it again.

A Healthy Intellectualism

Kerr is interested in the intellectual development of her readers. Wanting to arouse their curiosity, she drops in references to people and things that most teenagers would not have heard about. For example, in *Dinky Hocker Shoots Smack!* Tucker's mother tells him that as an artist he is "a depressing Bosch." To his questioning, she responds with the full name Hieronymus Bosch and tells Tucker to look him up, which he does: "A Dutch painter known for his scenes of nightmarish tortures in hell at the hands of weird monsters."

Tucker is one of Kerr's most openly intellectual protagonists. He writes a poem for English class but it is about the library and therefore he will never finish it or show it to anyone. "He was aware that a male cat-lover, who was also a lover of libraries, was better off keeping all that to himself." He plans to wait until college to announce his career plan of becoming a librarian, when he has just scored a winning touchdown or "won high honors in some course like Outer Space Cartography."

Tucker became an authority on libraries when he was in elementary school. His parents limited his television viewing, and so he spent hours reading and sketching in public libraries: "He went to them as often as drunks did to dry out and read up on their symptoms in the medical books; and as often as crazies did to talk to themselves in corners and warm themselves by radiators."

Tucker knew that "there were librarians and librarians," meaning some sat behind the information desk as if it were a moat that you dared not cross, others grilled you on whether you had looked in the card catalog or the 600 section, but then there were also the "ones who really knew where everything was, and the answer to every conceivable question, and ways to look up things which would shame and astonish Socrates, Plato, Solomon and Dr. Pangloss." Through Tucker, Kerr is saying that people are individuals, and even though they are doing the same jobs they will do them in tremendously different ways.

In *Is That You, Miss Blue?*, readers are treated to Miss Blue's best lectures on Antoine Henri Becquerel, Pierre Curie, and Marie Sklodowska Curie. In case someone really grows interested, Kerr also drops in the names of Sir J. J. Thomson and Sir Ernest Rutherford.

In 1964 Kerr published *Sudden Endings,* a nonfiction book about suicide. Some of the details that Kerr shares with young readers in her novels reflect a continuing interest in the topic of death. In *I Stay Near You,* for example, someone has to climb on the roof of the house the night that Grandfather Dechepare dies and bring down one of the tiles to the grandmother. It was an old Basque custom to enable the corpse's spirit to escape from the house and ascend to heaven.

In more than one book, Kerr refers to the beautifully written and humble "Death-Cell Prayer of Mary, Queen of Scots." The situation is full of the kind of irony that Kerr likes—a person condemned to execution by her own cousin is a model of love and forgiveness, at least in the prayer.

In *Is That You, Miss Blue?* Kerr teaches us macabre information through Sumner Thomas's conversations about suicide. During all the slow dances, he tells Flanders the intriguing details that he intends to put in a book called "Killing Yourself Successfully." As Sumner explains, it's not as easy as it seems. Artist Arshile Gorky "hung nooses all over his Connecticut property until he got the nerve to put his head through one." A psychologist named Stekel killed himself by swallowing twenty-two bottles of aspirin after he made a study of suicide. Sumner thinks that if he were to commit suicide he would jump because "It's still a very sure way," even though someone who does it is admitting that he thinks he has fallen from favor. The reason that Sumner is so preoccupied with suicide is that his mother, a very dramatic person, committed suicide on Christmas Eve and left a note saying "Everyone is to blame for this. Everyone who reads this note or hears about it."

Sumner would have probably enjoyed talking with Wally Witherspoon from *I'll Love You When You're More Like Me.* Wally writes an A+ essay on "Fear and Funerals" in which he points out that people do not really wear black out of respect for the dead, but instead to be inconspicuous, so that the ghost of the corpse won't notice them near the coffin and try to lure them to their deaths too. Coffins are carried out of the church feet first to keep the corpse from looking back and beckoning one of the family to follow. Long, exaggerated eulogies and flowers are given to appease the ghost, while the music and a handful of dirt tossed into the open grave are to lay its spirit to rest.

Wally's mortician father, on a scale of one to ten, ranks minus-one when it comes to curiosity about funeral superstitions. Wally figures that it is because he "still carries with him a lot of the old guilt undertakers used to have about the profession." Many of them would live in towns miles away from their mortuaries, and commute to work as if they were shopkeepers or salesmen.

The Sociology of Language

Kerr is a lover of words. She delights in their sounds and their double and triple meanings, and hence some of the most intriguing facts that she teaches us—through her characters' mouths—are about language. For example, in *The Son of Someone Famous,* Adam says, "I remember something my father once told me about the word 'crisis,' when it's written in Chinese. It's composed of two characters: One represents danger and the other represents opportunity." In *ME ME ME ME ME,* Marijane, in an argument announces "That's an untruth," and then explains, decades before Watergate, that this was what her grandmother always called a lie.

One of the funniest scenes in *Little Little* occurs when Sydney is called into the principal's office and scolded for singing his theme song "La cucaracha" in a school assembly.

> "You're some kind of a smart aleck, aren't you, Cinnamon?"
> "What do you mean, sir?"
> "Singing about marihuana that way."
> "That's the song," I said. "I didn't make up the words."
> "You didn't make up porque la falta, marihuana que fumar?"
> "That's the song" I said "La Cucaracha, la cucaracha, doesn't want to travel on because she hasn't marihuana for to smoke."

In spite of the explanation, Sydney suspects that the principal does not believe him because he thinks marihuana is some new weed discovered in the seventies. Therefore it couldn't be referred to in a song written decades ago.

The number of people who sang the song in the 1950s never giving a thought to the meaning of the lyrics is a wonderful illustration of how oblivious people can be to the world around them— even to the things they themselves say, or in this case sing. Kerr does not want her readers sleepwalking through life in this fashion.

No character expounds linguistic insights better than Wally in *I'll Love You When You're More Like Me*. His teacher, Mr. Sponzini, says he would make a good etymologist or linguist, but Wally's father does not appreciate it when Wally spouts out a Latin quote from the Roman naturalist Pliny the Elder exploring the similarities between orchids and testicles. Nor does his mother appreciate the essay he writes on linguistic evasions that was inspired by her euphemisms for death. The essay explains that Indonesian has no world for *tiger* because the people are afraid the word might summon one, that in Madagascar people avoid the word *lightning* lest it strike, that Russian peasants try to placate their enemy the bear by calling it "honey eater," and that in Hungary it used to be common to tell mothers how ugly their new babies were in order to avoid arousing the jealousy of evil spirits.

When Wally first meets Sabra St. Amour on the beach and she asks him for a cigarette, Kerr establishes Wally's cleverness with the following antismoking message: "You'd have to be a little crazy to let the tobacco companies manipulate you. . . . Why do you think they'd name a cigarette something like Merit? Merit's supposed to mean excellence, value, reward. What's so excellent, valuable and rewarding about having cancer?" Sabra's flip reply is that she's heard of coming to the beach for some sun, a swim, or even a walk, but never for a lecture. Wally is undaunted, realizing that he has stumbled onto an idea that isn't half-bad. He goes on with "Vantage—as in advantage; True; More; Now. . . . Live for the moment because you won't live long. Get More. Be True to your filthy habit."

Sabra's response keeps this from sounding like adult-sponsored moralizing. But even if readers interpret it as a health rather than a linguistics lesson, they are not likely to feel preached at because they are involved in understanding Wally's point.

Of Writers and Writing

Another reason that Kerr does not appear didactic is that she chooses to teach about things she sincerely believes in. She is interested in authors and in literature and she wants young people to share her enthusiasm. In the worlds she creates, people produce letters, notes, want ads, one-liners, press releases, newspapers, and even books. The characters who are good writers turn out to be winners. In *If I Love You, Am I Trapped Forever?* Duncan Stein, alias Doomed, transforms the social structure of Cayuta High through the newspaper *Remote,* which he founds and edits. At the end of *Little Little,* humpbacked Sydney is shown to be a winner when the English teacher chooses to read aloud his story rather than Calpurnia Dove's or Little Little's. In *Gentlehands,* the investigative reporter, despite his obnoxious personality, is proven right. And in *I Stay Near You,* the ending is optimistic in part because Vincent's son thinks he is falling in love with the teenage writer who lives next door.

In *Love Is a Missing Person,* Suzy says about "a dippy-looking girl" with white hair that she always wants to read something she's written to the class, and "She's so sure of herself when it comes to her own work, . . . you become unsure about your original judgment of the rest of her." Kerr also reveals her empathy for young writers in *I'll Love You When You're More Like Me.* Wally's little sister, A. E., is an aspiring poet who is constantly seeking praise by reading aloud something she has written. She reads a poem to Wally and tells him it is by Emily Dickinson. After he responds to her questions about it by saying, "It's fine," A. E. triumphantly announces that she is the real author. When he doesn't act appropriately impressed, A. E. bitterly complains that if you say Emily Dickinson or Sylvia Plath or Edna St. Vincent Millay wrote it then "Everyone swoons over it. If you say you wrote it, you get screwed."

Katherine Paterson, Newbery Award winning author of *Bridge to Terabithia, The Great Gilly Hopkins,* and *Jacob Have I Loved,* has confessed to performing this same trick when she was a child.

Probably most of the writer-related incidents that Kerr includes are outgrowths of her own experience. For example, after she became a respected YA author, English teachers and librarians whispered about "what Kerr used to *have* to write." They were referring to the romances and thrillers she wrote under various pen names. It is that kind of attitude that Tucker's father displays in *Dinky Hocker Shoots Smack!* when he instructs Tucker to tell people that his mother writes for Arrow Publications rather than Stirring Romances.

An incident in *If I Love You, Am I Trapped Forever?* also shows an insider's view of the writer's world. Alan goes to New York to meet the father he has never known. He tells his dad he is going to be a writer. Alan's dad is pleased and says he does some writing himself—advertising writing, he adds in an apologetic tone. Instead of graciously accepting his dad's humility, Alan interrupts to say that he is not going to be a commercial writer. The father gets even by asking Alan if he is going to be another Thomas Wolfe, and when Alan does not quite hear him, he insults Alan by changing the reference to J. D. Salinger.

Because of the wide popularity of *Catcher in the Rye,* Salinger is one of the few authors that most teenagers know. Kerr uses this common knowledge to show that Valerie Kissenwiser in *Him She Loves?* is more sophisticated than the average student. Valerie tells Henry that she hopes to work in publishing or to write a novel. When Valerie says she loves Joan Didion, Henry says he does, too, even though he has never heard of her. To get back on familiar ground, he changes the subject to J. D. Salinger. Valerie responds in a yawning tone, "Oh, Salinger. All the assassins in the world are going around with *Catcher in the Rye* in their back pockets!"

As part of her enthusiasm for writers and writing, Kerr sprinkles literary references throughout her books. For example, in *Dinky Hocker Shoots Smack!* authors Ashley Montagu, Horace Walpole, and Maxim Gorky are briefly mentioned. Tucker and Natalia are drawn together by a line from St. Exupery's *The Little Prince.* Kerr probably took this idea from her nonfiction book on suicide, in which she tells how Marilyn Monroe once gave Joe

DiMaggio a gold medal for his watch chain engraved with a line from *The Little Prince*: "True love is visible not to the eyes, but to the heart, for eyes may be deceived." DiMaggio wondered "what the hell it meant."

Kerr, who is a master at making her point with just the right quotation, was a little insulted when asked in the interview if, like Suzy's new stepmother in *Love Is a Missing Person*, she relies on books of quotations. She said the only time she refers to such references is as a last-minute check on the accuracy of her memory. She is a voracious reader, and when she runs across something she likes she either memorizes it or makes a note.

In *Love Is a Missing Person*, Carl Sandburg, Emily Dickinson, Oscar Wilde, Gertrude Stein, and Josephine Tey (Miss Spring's favorite dead mystery writer) are cited. In *Is That You, Miss Blue?* the headmistress uses a line from Ralph Waldo Emerson to lecture Flanders, but Agnes goes her one better when she tapes a quote from D. H. Lawrence on the mirror in the bathroom where Miss Blue has hung the crucifixion picture:

I worship Christ, I worship Jehovah, I worship Pan, I worship Aphrodite.
But I do not worship hands nailed and running with blood upon a cross.

In *I'll Love You When You're More Like Me*, Harriet Hren responds to the impending break-up with Wally by quoting George Bernard Shaw: "When a prisoner (which you claim you've been, Wally) sees the door of his dungeon open, he dashes for it without stopping to think where he shall get his dinner outside."

In *If I Love You, Am I Trapped Forever?* Alan feels a bit of empathy for his father when just after Alan wrote a theme on Father Time's destruction, his father quotes a line from Tennessee Williams about time being the enemy of all of us. He also gets a surprising insight into his mother when he overhears her defend his long-absent father. She says that he left the family out of weakness rather than meanness, and she quotes from Williams's *Cat on a Hot Tin Roof*, "Oh, you weak, beautiful people who give up with such grace. What you need is someone to take hold of you—gently with love, and hand your life back to you."

Later in the book as a humorous light touch, Catherine Stein quotes an O. Henry line and tells Alan she used to go to a restaurant in New York called Pete's where O. Henry would sit at a table and write his stories. Alan asks her if she ever met him and then is embarrassed when she laughs and says she's not quite that "long in the tooth."

A Course in Psychology

Anyone who has read Kerr's books has the equivalent of at least the first six weeks of a course in basic psychology because Kerr puts into words many of the vague feelings that her readers do not have the sophistication to describe. Yet, when they read something like Brenda Belle's confession of insecurity in *The Son of Someone Famous,* they experience a jolt of recognition. Brenda Belle is puzzling over why Adam Blessing seems to like her and sadly concludes that it is because there's something wrong with him. He was probably expelled from school because he is "slightly crazy . . . whacked out." This depresses Brenda Belle because she was looking for "normal companionship, not a misfit. I wanted someone who fit, so I'd feel I fit, too."

There's really nothing wrong with Adam's head, but he too is looking suspiciously at his relationship with Brenda Belle—they're never affectionate with each other except in public. He tells his grandfather that he guesses he feels sorry for Brenda, and Mr. Blessing responds, "Don't let that be the only reason you want to see a girl. When you pity someone, sometimes all it means is you wish someone would pity you."

When Adam Blessing overhears his veterinarian grandfather giving out free advice over the telephone, he suddenly feels a surge of love for the old man, "because no matter what life had done to him, he wasn't mean." This impresses Adam because he has imagined that life doesn't have a lot of goodies in store for him either, and he isn't sure he can make it through without being mean. There have been times when he felt the meanness creeping into his soul, times when he "wanted to hurt someone, wanted someone to have a party where no one would show up . . . things like that."

Patricia Runk Sweeney said in an article published in *The Lion and the Unicorn* that Kerr's protagonists are all looking for "love for the hidden, needy person inside of them." They want "a love that lets them be" and relationships in which other characters recognize their strengths and weaknesses."[13]

When I quoted this to Kerr and asked for her response, she said that an author isn't in as good a position to look at the total picture of her own work and to make generalizations as is a careful and perceptive reader. But she did agree that she looks on love as a tremendous motivation, "especially important to young people because this is when they are the most involved and the most frightened, especially if it's a first love."

When Kerr writes about sex, she does not treat the obvious "should we" or "shouldn't we" questions. Instead she approaches the issue from a variety of unexpected angles, paying more attention to the emotional than the physical aspects. Early in *If I Love You, Am I Trapped Forever?* Alan sums up Kerr's philosophy when he writes:

The thing is: I'm not going to describe in detail the very personal things that take place between me and Leah. I'm not writing this book for a bunch of voyeurs. I'm tired of books written for voyeurs. Go out and get your own experience, any of you voyeurs who happen to be reading this. It's a story about people and how their minds work, not a story about how their bodies work.

Critic Robert Unsworth, writing in *School Library Journal*,[14] conjectured that it wasn't voyeurs but censors that Kerr was avoiding. However, his explanation does not stand up when looked at alongside all the other controversial topics that Kerr treats. A more likely explanation is that Kerr feels that the mass media, including many books and magazines for teenagers, already focus enough attention on the physical aspects of sexuality. She chooses to make her books stand out as different by taking the more challenging route of exploring subtle emotions rather than overt sexual behavior.

Even though in each book there is a boy/girl relationship, it is one of friendship as much as romance. Kerr shows her readers that not all relationships are the same and that not all teenagers have dates every Saturday night. Even one of the beautiful people, Sabra St. Amour in *I'll Love You When You're More Like Me,* confesses that she could write a book like the one she saw, *All about Sex after Fifty,* which was made up of nothing but blank pages. Sabra would entitle her book "What I Know about Boys."

When Sabra muses over how strained her conversations are with Wally compared to those with Charlie, whom she feels she could tell anything, she decides that her shrink would probably point out that it is because she doesn't have anything to fear from Charlie because he is gay. Then for the benefit of readers not privileged to have their own shrinks, Sabra adds, "My shrink didn't do a lot of pointing out—they don't, they mostly listen, which is why analysis goes on for years."

Kerr encourages her readers to look behind the surface structure of even the simplest actions. For example, when Wally, Charlie, and Harriet see Sabra at the local beach hangout, Harriet sends Wally over to ask Sabra for a dance. Wally ponders, "I'm not sure whether Harriet wanted to impress other people with the fact I'd met her, or whether she wanted to sit out a set with Charlie so he wouldn't leave us without wheels."

In *Is That You, Miss Blue?* Flanders is feeling guilty about making fun of Miss Blue and she says: "I had the feeling if I laughed any longer I'd have some terrible punishment inflicted on me, because I had the feeling what I was doing was cruel. My father had told me once that often if you did something cruel, you hurt yourself, had a trivial accident, or missed an appointment you looked forward to—as a way of making yourself pay for the cruelty." Flanders's father added his own little lecture at the end, "But there is no God up there deciding you're not going to get this because you did that!"

Of Skepticism and Zeal

Kerr's bravery in including such a statement is evident only to someone familiar enough with young adult literature to realize how neglected God and religion are in teenage fiction. Young adult authors have shied away from writing about religion because publishers have resisted such books on the grounds that public school teachers and librarians have hesitated to buy them. The result has been a general neglect. It is similar to what Reverend Martin E. Marty, a religion professor at the University of Chicago, noted in an article for *TV Guide*, "We Need More Religion in Our Sitcoms." He feels that "It is artificial, almost eerie, to see characters like George and Louise Jefferson of *The Jeffersons*, Arthur (the Fonz) Fonzarelli of *Happy Days* or Klinger's Korean war bride Soon-Lee of *AfterM*A*S*H* cut off from their roots and the religion that would very likely be a large part of their lives in real life."[15]

The absence of religion from young adult books is especially unrealistic since for many people the teenage years are the ones in which they spend the most time and energy thinking about and discussing religion. As part of developing their independence, they have to make religious decisions, deciding for example, whether to stay with the faith (or nonfaith) of their parents, whether to approach religion as whole-hearted believers, skeptics, or something in between. This is a dilemma that Kerr understands, and throughout her books she continues to make intriguing observations that give readers something to ponder. She does not point her audience toward any particular belief or nonbelief system, but simply communicates that religious matters deserve some prime-time thinking.

In *ME ME ME ME ME*, she writes that she comes from a religious background, having attended an Episcopalian boarding school and having an aunt who was a Roman Catholic nun. Yet Kerr says that she always seemed to have a quarrel with organized religion, probably because she quarreled with any kind of authority. She writes:

Religion still fascinates me, whether it's a book by Paul Tillich, a local church service, a seder I'm invited to by Jewish friends, a talk with a Moonie on the street, a Billy Graham appearance, or one of the Sunday-morning TV preachers. I don't yet "believe"—and some of what I see I love or hate, but I'm rarely indifferent, which leaves me more involved than not.

It is interesting that Kerr confesses her lack of "belief" in the autobiographical *ME ME ME ME ME,* because in her novels she is careful to present a variety of opinions or no opinion at all—just reminders that religion is a part of life.

In her first book, Dinky Hocker cleverly announces that the biblical theme for the day is boredom. When Tucker argues that "There's nothing about boredom in the Bible," Dinky responds that he wouldn't know since he and his family "only show up in church once a year." Finally Dinky explains that her biblical theme is taken from Hebrews 13:8, "Jesus Christ the same yesterday, and today, and forever."

The morning after Tucker's family's health food store burns, Tucker writes P. John that they are all going to church and "pray like mad for a miracle." As the minister intones, "Almighty God, the fountain of all wisdom, who knowest our necessities before we ask, and our weaknesses before we sin; we beseech thee to forgive and have compassion upon our infirmities . . . ," Tucker looks over at his uncle and can't figure out if his face is so red because of the references to weaknesses, forgiveness, and infirmities or because he has his usual Sunday-morning hangover.

Three books later in *Is That You, Miss Blue?* religion takes a front seat. Besides the obvious irony of Miss Blue's being dismissed from teaching at a church-sponsored school because she is "too" religious, there are the scenes showing how deprived Cardmaker is because her father's ministerial salary does not stretch far enough to buy her a winter coat or a party dress. After the big dance of the year, Cardmaker is punished for being found in the bathroom with a boy. All she was trying to do was wash off the purple that had gotten on her neck from her newly dyed but very old dress. She would rather be expelled from school than confess the truth to her father, who already feels guilty about being a poor provider.

The family got into their financial situation when Cardmaker's father took it upon himself to point out things he was dissatisfied with in the church, and a certain Right Reverend (who took the "right" in his title literally) had him transferred to the poorest parish in New Jersey. This leaves Cardmaker fuming over "a bunch of phonies living off stories of Jesus," a poor man who did not even have a title but today is represented by men "hustling to get the rich parishes with the big houses and long black cars" and wanting "to be the Right Reverend this and the Holiness that. . . ."

The way the world ignores the underside of religion is epitomized by the scene in which Cute Diblee's newly rich but unsophisticated father comes to pick up the girls to take them out for dinner. Headmistress Anna P. Ettinger typically pretends not to hear a word that Mr. Dibblee says in answer to Mrs. Ettinger's statement that Cardmaker cannot leave the campus because she is being disciplined.

Well, who among us don't have sin, as the Bible says? Some of the greatest saints were sinners, ma'am. Moses murdered an Egyptian and hid him in the sand; David was an adulterer who took away the wives of three men; Jacob was a liar and a thief, deceived his blind and aging papa so he could get something didn't belong to him . . . and old Mary Magdalene was a hooker.

Cute is so embarrassed that she turns pale while Flanders has to "concentrate on national disasters to keep from laughing."

The running argument that the school girls have about atheism and agnosticism gives Kerr the opportunity to bring in several opposing opinions. The most extreme statement that Flanders can bring herself to make is that she is "maybe an agnostic," to which Cardmaker responds, "That's the trouble with you agnostics. You're so damn wishy-washy and jelly-spined. Maybe this and maybe that." Earlier in church, Flanders sat by a girl who sang the hymn backwards:

"Why are you singing it backwards?" I whispered.

"Because religion is backwards," she answered.

Then Flanders remembers Cardmaker's vow to start an atheist club and correctly guesses that the girl belongs.

"How can you be an atheist when your mother owns a white Mercedes?" I said.

"A Mercedes has nothing to do with God."

"How can you *not* believe in God with all you have?" I persisted. "Atheism is for have-nots and malcontents."

"You know nothing about atheists," she said. "A lot of us are worth fortunes."

"Way your it have." I shrugged.

Topping off a scene with a little joke like this is typical of how Kerr gets away with making serious points without leaving her readers feeling preached at. She also lets her characters go away with varying opinions. For example, although Cardmaker finally decides to "take God back," Flanders appears to remain basically the same agnostic throughout.

Even in books whose plots do not center around religion, Kerr includes some intriguing references to religious matters. In *I'll Love You When You're More Like Me,* Sabra shows how different she is from the local townspeople by describing Charlie's living room with its gun case, plastic palm tree, and machine-made wall sampler advising that "Religion should be our steering wheel, not our spare tire."

In the same book, Kerr makes her first reference to television evangelism when Sabra explains that on Sundays her mother never comes out of her bedroom until Dr. Robert Schuller's sermon on television. She describes him as a little blue-eyed bespectacled man preaching positive thinking while the television cameras show "thoughtful faces, flower arrangements, the trees outside, fountains and people sitting in parked cars listening to him."

In *Little Little,* Sydney Cinammon confesses that although

prayer was not a regular part of his routine, he had been known to pray in times of crisis such as when being attacked by a bulldog during a Fourth of July parade. Sydney mentions this in connection with a story he tells about the time he and his cottage mates from the home for handicapped children attended a revival meeting where the evangelist asked people to testify to what the Lord had done for them.

People began getting up and shouting out they'd been changed or cured or transformed overnight. Then there was a lull in the proceedings . . . then Wheel's voice. He raised himself as high as he could on his board, and he yelled, "You was asking what the Lord done for me! So I'll tell you! He blamed near ruint me."

This story is a prelude to the bigger role that religion plays in the book that contrasts the ministries of Sydney's scheming friend, Little Lion (formerly known as Opportunity Knox), and Little Little's wise and kindly grandfather. It is this kind of contrast that fascinates Kerr and becomes the main theme in *What I Really Think of You.* Protagonist Opal Ringer, whose father is the pitifully poor pentecostal preacher, expresses the doubts that most people at least occasionally feel when she confesses that if given the choice between being part of "The Rapture" and being one of the "haves," the kids going by in their cars, some with tops down, tape decks playing, and hair flying in the wind, she would have to "wrestle sons of Satan" to make the right decision. The whole idea of the Rapture frightens Opal because she is afraid that when God comes down to take her back up with him, she will "be caught in my true thoughts like a cat with my paw in the fishbowl."

Critic Kathy Piehl, writing on "The Business of Religion in M. E. Kerr's Books," expressed the idea that Kerr puts more passion into her writing about religion than into her writing about sex and implied that the religious fervor may in fact be a substitute for sexuality. For example, Jesse Pegler gets goose bumps when he hears the first chorus of "Farther Along" and knows that this is the cue for his father to come out and blast the audience "sky-high with his preaching." On warm nights Opal aches with a longing for "nothing that she knows about," and when any one of the "haves" shows up at her father's church to see "how the holy rollers roll" she feels like she's walking around in front of people in her underwear. She is embarrassed for herself, "the speck of my dream that doesn't know about the glow coming."

Kerr said Piehl's theory had surprised her because she had not intended sexual connotations. She was telling a story and was interested in communicating the charisma of religion, "but there is a valid point in the similarity of any expression of joy whether it stems from religion or something else."

"It's harder to write about religion than sex," Kerr went on to lament. "With religion you can't please *anybody*." Kerr was also surprised that in Piehl's discussion of *Little Little* she left out "the one sensible person in the book"—Grandfather La Belle, the Methodist minister who was the only one smart enough to see that Little Little could not be kept under glass her whole life.

Family Relationships

In *ME ME ME ME ME*, Kerr writes about going through a period in which her family seemed nothing but an embarrassment.

Why did my mother wear so much junk jewelry? Why did my father have to say things like "Soup's on!" instead of "Dinner's ready," or "How do?" instead of "How do you do?" Why did my mother have to mention the price of everything, and talk about "bargains?" Why didn't we ever have wine with dinner, or go to concerts, and why did my father have to call classical music "long-hair noise?"

Marijane was glad that she chose to go to boarding school a long way from home and that because of the war, travel was curtailed and her family wouldn't be coming to visit and humiliate her.

That Kerr remembers these negative feelings so well gives her an advantage in writing for young people who are just beginning

to experience them. Some of what Kerr says about family relationships is pretty obvious, but she puts everyday disagreements
into different contexts from those that her readers are accustomed to. For example, in *What I Really Think of You,* every Sunday Opal is irritated with her preacher father. After the family
comes home from church, while she and her mother prepare dinner, he goes into his room and prays out loud about all the things
sitting "heavy on his head like a basket of wet wash." Most of
these things relate to the activities of individual family members.
When company comes for dinner it is especially embarrassing,
"like going to the toilet with the door open." One particular day,
when Opal had been begging to be allowed to go to a costume
party, Reverend Ringer prays that Opal will "cast her eyes from
this godless astrology." Opal's mother, Arnelle, tries to smooth her
feelings and tell her not to be critical of her father, but then the
prayer goes on, "Jesus, help Arnelle fight Satan's gluttony so's she
can sing your praises once again before our humble flock, guide
her from. . . ." Opal's mother isn't nearly so understanding about
this prayer and Opal can't resist adding to her mother's discom-
fort by saying "Shoe's on the other foot now"—an especially satisfying remark for young readers who have experienced this kind
of familial double standard.

At other times Kerr writes of more subtle conflicts. Alan in *If I
Love You, Am I Trapped Forever?* explains how his grandfather is
a put-down artist—not the kind who would say anything like
"Alan, you stupid clown, nobody wants to read anything you'd
write!" Instead he would say something like "Well, it's a big undertaking. I hope you can pull it off," or "Just remember, you put
all that time and money into the boat you were going to build,
and nothing came of *that* either."

Little Little focuses more on family relationships than do several of the other books where the protagonists are single children
with single parents. Because of Little Little's dwarfism, the family is bonded together against the inquisitive stares of strangers
and the world's prejudice against anyone different; nevertheless
there's ample tension, which Mrs. La Belle prefers to call bickering. Little Little and her sister Cowboy have an interesting con-

versation about family ties in which Little Little confesses that she thinks that by being born a dwarf, she ruined the charmed life her parents had led in their youth. Cowboy argues that it was simply that her parents grew up, "Nothing good begins with 'adult.' There's adult, adulterate, adultery. . . ." Besides, Cowboy goes on to argue, "They ruined yours. It was the combination of the two of them that made you what you are, wasn't it?" Then she rushes to add, "Not that what you are is bad."

Most of Kerr's themes are slightly off the beaten path. Like a frontier housewife who saves dough from one batch of bread to use as starter's yeast for the next batch, she has taken some of the most interesting minor points from her earlier books and expanded them in her later ones. For example, in *What I Really Think of You,* when Jesse Pegler's family talks about missing older brother Bud, who ran away on Jesse's sixteenth birthday, Mrs. Pegler says to the father, "You have to share your missing him with others who miss him too. When you can't do that, we've got two people to miss, Bud and you." This is reminiscent of the theme of *Love Is a Missing Person,* as well as of a telephone conversation between Suzy's mother and her former husband. Barry Slade is apparently talking to his ex-wife about his upcoming marriage to Enid and he says, "I wish I could just get out of it, escape it, go to Mexico or some damn place and become a missing person." Evelyn Slade responds in her own melancholy tone, "Oh, Barry, don't you realize that you already *are* a missing person."

Kerr's cross-generational stories such as *I Stay Near You* and *The Son of Someone Famous* provide the kind of gossip that traditionally taught folk values and expectations to young people growing up in the less mobile, rural societies of an earlier time. Along with such teaching, Kerr throws in a grain of skepticism. In *The Son of Someone Famous,* Brenda's mother says about Christine Cutler that she "is no one to look up to, believe me. I know things about her father that are repulsive and revolting." Brenda's mother does not intend to repeat them, but as she warns, "you can take my word . . . and blood will always tell."

The statement proves to have some truth to it, but not in the way that Brenda's mother thinks. Instead of supporting her idea that Christine is not good enough for Adam, it explains their mutual attraction in that Adam's mother and Christine's father had been in love with each other.

In one of the most sincere-sounding moments in *ME ME ME ME ME,* Kerr tells how on a summer job she could listen in on the town's telephone conversations hearing not only her girlfriends gossiping, but also her mother sharing intimate details of the Meaker household. She learns more than she wants to know—for example, that Mrs. Meaker suspects her husband of having an affair with his secretary, that she has her third child in hopes of keeping her husband interested in family life, and that she thinks Marijane writes so much because it is her way of hiding from self-consciousness about her long nose. "Up until that moment, I hadn't thought my nose was all that long . . . and so I'd been given something to think about—obsess about—appropriate punishment, perhaps, for my snooping."

This lesson that in the real world punishment is a natural follow-up for breaking rules rather than something artificially concocted for the benefit of the young is spelled out more clearly than most of Kerr's lessons. Usually she has her characters make observations from which readers are free to draw lessons, but she doesn't insist. For example in *Love Is a Missing Person,* Suzy's new stepmother, Enid, offers to let Suzy borrow a swimsuit even though it is obvious that she cannot fit into it. When Suzy says, "Thanks anyway. The sun isn't a big deal to me, since I live right on the ocean," she realizes that she is "being a little bitchy." Kerr leaves it at this, but she hopes that her readers will figure out that Suzy's surliness is her way of getting even with Enid for being more vain than considerate. Kerr does not imply that this is either right or wrong. What she wants is for readers to begin to look at their own reasons for behaving in certain ways.

A Woman's Place

Feminism is a social issue that frequently finds its way into Kerr's books. Marijane learns her first lesson in the power of boys, according to *ME ME ME ME ME,* at Laura Bryan's ballroom dancing school where

> You couldn't even get out on the floor without a boy choosing you for a partner. If a boy didn't choose you, you were a wallflower, which was a poor wretch, all dressed up, sitting by herself on the sidelines in a folding chair, pretending she was fascinated by her own hands.
> Boys were never wallflowers.

A less obvious feminist statement appears in *Love Is a Missing Person* when Kerr has Suzy discover that Mr. Slade never really asks about Suzy's sister. Instead he is only concerned with how she feels about him, "as though apart from that she had no existence which was of any importance."

In *What I Really Think of You,* Seal von Hennig gets her nickname from becoming the St. Francis of Seaville High when she dates Eddie Eden, whose father runs an animal preserve. "Seal always got gung ho on any subject that interested the boy she was dating. She was known for that around Seaville."

In *Little Little,* the characters argue openly about careers vs. motherhood, as do Brenda Belle and her mother in *The Son of Someone Famous.* Brenda's mother is always drawing comparisons between Brenda and her Aunt Faith, who in her youth "was very busy being the smart aleck, slapping her knees when she laughed, getting to her feet in company to mimic someone," just never thinking how she looked to boys. Aunt Faith finally married, but her husband "never gave her a child." Brenda explains, "My mother always said a man *gave* a woman a child, as though the woman had no part in its conception."

The irony of this attitude is stronger when compared to what happens in *Is That You, Miss Blue?* The most popular girl in school, France Shipp, does not come back after Christmas. The rumor is that she is pregnant, but her boyfriend is back at the neighboring boys' school, "as handsome as ever, showing no signs of being involved. . . ."

Little Little is impressed that when Tom Thumb died he was buried in a big, fancy vault with a grandiose epitaph, while right next to it, on Lavinia Thumb's vault, the only message was "His Wife," not even her name. Lavinia had been two inches shorter than Tom. When Little Little asked her grandfather where all the famous female dwarfs were, "he said they were buried in history along with other notable ladies." But she did find one to write her senior research paper on, Lia Graf, the twenty-seven-inch circus performer who had her picture taken sitting on the lap of J. P. Morgan when he was testifying before the Senate Banking Committee.

Kerr manages to include such incidents without offending nonfeminist readers because she shines the spotlight on them for only a sentence or two and then moves quickly on. She does not tell her readers what their response should be. And when it is deserved, she will throw in a counterargument to balance the scales. The best example of this is in *I'll Love You When You're More Like Me*. Wally reminds his little sister "for the umpteenth time" that she could be the one to carry on the family mortuary business. She responds that she plans to be "an internationally renowned poet, and besides it isn't woman's work." "Where is women's liberation when I need it?" Wally plaintively asks.

Even though Kerr identifies with the feminists of the 1980s, she grew up in the 1940s and 1950s, and was undoubtedly influenced by national attitudes as well as by those of her own family and region. This may be one of the reasons that the fathers in her books are so much splashier and more interesting than the mothers. Early in *What I Really Think of You*, Jesse Pegler says, "The most important thing about me has always been who my father is." In *Love Is a Missing Person*, Suzy says, "I wasn't the only one who thought my dad was something special. It was all spelled out in any *Who's Who*, in write-ups in *Business Week, Fortune*; even *Sunday Interview* had televised half an hour on him." In *Is That You, Miss Blue?* Flanders won't date a boy who describes her father as "the answer to the question: What does the duck say? (Quack, quack, quack)." And even after a television show proves the boy right, she gets a consoling note from her friend that ends with "P. S. Your father's great-looking."

In *The Son of Someone Famous*, Adam goes by his mother's

maiden name so that people won't expect as much from him as they do from his famous father. In *Him She Loves?* and *I Stay Near You,* the fathers are in show business. On a national scale, they are only moderately successful, but they are still the kinds of celebrities who qualify as beautiful people living in the fast lane. If *Gentlehands* is added to this list, then in more than half of Kerr's books, the plot is advanced through the young protagonists reading or hearing about their famous male progenitors in the mass media.

When I questioned Kerr about how much more excitingly she paints fathers than mothers, she explained that she was a "daddy's girl." This relationship was typical of families in the 1940s and 1950s. If she wanted to borrow the car, she would wheedle permission out of her father; if her brothers wanted something, they would go to their mother. As a feminist, Kerr said that she still has a lot of consciousness raising to do herself. For example, when she was recently talking about stocks with a woman friend, and wanting to get agreement on a point she was making, she told the woman to "go home and ask Charlie [the woman's husband] about it."

"If I could understand it," Kerr sheepishly explained, "there's no reason that my friend couldn't also."

Even though the mothers in Kerr's books pale when compared to the fathers, developing their characters may have required as much from Kerr as did creating the "star" stereotypes who were the fathers. A few of the mothers, such as Little Little's pretentious and foolish mother, who prides herself on writing a poem in an afternoon, and Dinky Hocker's who sees everyone's problems but those of her own daughter, are just as shallow as the cardboard fathers. But for every mother like them, there is also one who lives and breathes the stuff of real life.

The critics who correctly pointed out that the portrayal of Dinky Hocker's mother was too negative to be believed, in fairness should have also mentioned that Tucker's mother was an ideal and believable blend of common sense, understanding, and ambition. Tucker finding his mother asleep at the kitchen table where she was trying to study is a memorable scene. He later confides his amazement to Natalia when he realizes that his mother wants to be something more significant than just his mother. A similar idea appears in *Is That You, Miss Blue?* when Flanders is giving her mother a sermon on parental responsibility and her mother says, "Flan, I have news for you. I didn't give up my right to individuality once I had you."

In *Love Is a Missing Person,* Suzy Slade's mother is a multifaceted character, who at first seems frivolous, dressing to match her sun porch and wanting to prove that she can win back her husband even though she does not want him. But as the book progresses, she is shown to have considerable depth. She makes Suzy go to work at the library on the day that her sister runs away, explaining, "In a crisis, you do the same as you do every day. That's what holds things together. Routine is fiber, and in a crisis, fiber binds." Mrs. Slade also helps Suzy understand that she is projecting her own resentment toward her sister when she fears that Chicago is going to do something dreadful to her.

But in spite of such wisdom and understanding, Mrs. Slade does not become too wise or too good to be believed. She is catty about the woman her former husband decides to marry, and she resents it when one of her friends attributes the mismatch to love rather than to a psychotic condition on the part of Mr. Slade.

On Being Different

Kerr gives her readers glimpses of the many faces of prejudice. Her goal is not to sermonize, but to help readers recognize that prejudice is very much a part of most people's lives and that overcoming it is a personal challenge. Thoughtful readers of *Dinky Hocker Shoots Smack!* will question their own prejudices against either political liberals or conservatives, fat people, those who have been institutionalized for mental-health problems, and people who have been on drugs. Prejudices based on socioeconomic differences can be almost as strong as those based on race, a point well illustrated in *I'll Love You When You're More Like Me, Gentle-hands, What I Really Think of You,* and *The Son of Someone Famous.*

In *Is That You, Miss Blue?* Kerr uses common stereotypes to make a point about prejudices against handicapped people. She shows how the deaf Agnes and the asthmatic Flanders are isolated and then overprotected. The absurdity of putting them together in an out-of-the-way dormitory with only Miss Blue for companionship may go unnoticed by some readers, but Kerr makes sure no one will miss the ridiculousness of Agnes's being fixed up with a blind date who is actually blind.

The prejudice that Kerr is the most comfortable writing about, probably because she has observed it the most closely, is anti-Semitism. In *If I Love You, Am I Trapped Forever?* Alan's grandfather never allows him to say that someone is Jewish. He insists that it is more polite to say "of the Jewish persuasion." Once a year in Cayuta, Rabbi Goldman gives the Sunday sermon at the Second Presbyterian Church, and once a year Reverend Gosnell addresses the Saturday congregation at Temple Emmanuel. Still Jews are not numbered among the members of the Cayuta North Country Club even though they control the Yacht Club, and "No one's exactly pushing for intermarriage. . . ." Kerr's point is that prejudice is not limited to the seamier sides of life.

In *Little Little,* black Calpurnia Dove and Little Little are in the same English class and compete as writers. When Miss Grossman reads aloud something that Calpurnia has written, Little Little thinks that Miss Grossman is only being nice to Calpurnia because she is black. But Little Little is mature enough to realize that when something she has written gets read aloud, Calpurnia probably "decides Miss Grossman is only being nice to me because I'm a dwarf." Little Little explains that most of the black teenagers in La Belle go to Commercial High to learn business skills or trades. "Of the few that go to La Belle High, one is always elected to some office, unanimously. But that high honor rarely gets one of them a seat saved at noon in the cafeteria among the whites, or even a particularly warm hello."

One of Calpurnia Dove's essays that Miss Grossman reads includes the following:

The first time I was ever called nigger I was four years old and went home crying. Didn't even know why I was, didn't even know what "nigger" meant. Only knew it was bad. So my mother say oh they got around to saying that to you, did they, well get in the boat here along with the rest of us, you got a lot of company on the stormy sea, honey, ain't one of us not been called that, ain't one of us heard "nigger" for the last time, either.

Little Little longs for company and tells of daydreaming that she is from an all-dwarf family, "mother, father, grandparents, and Cowboy all shrunk to my size, living in a little house locked in against a larger world, laughing at them and cursing them, sharing their tyranny with other La Belles."

When Little Little's grandfather takes her to a convention of dwarfs, she is amazed that "coming into view, coming out of cars and around the sides of cars, falling from the heavens for all I knew, were others like me, redheaded, blond, blue-eyed, brown-eyed, straight, twisted, beautiful, ugly, in-between: a world of me." The first person that Little Little speaks to is the beautiful, four-foot, one-inch Eloise Ficklin, who snubs Little Little. Afterwards, as Little Little gets acquainted with the others, they explain tht Eloise never makes friends with dwarfs who are perfectly formed. She is what's called a repudiator. Although her parents make her come to the conventions, she likes to pretend that she is just short and so she picks out the kids who aren't like her at all and then acts as though she is helping them out. "The more you're like her," they explain, "the less she'll like you." When Little Little relates the incident to her grandfather that night, he says:

Well, you have learned something about prejudice today, Little Little. The person at the top of the ladder doesn't pick on the one way at the bottom. He picks on the one on the rung next to him. The fellow way at the bottom picks on the fellow on the ground. There's always someone to look down on, if looking down on someone is your style.

Little Little swears that she will never treat anyone that way, but Grandfather La Belle assures her that "no one looks up all the time. When things get tough people drop their eyes. The crucial thing is to remember to raise them back up before you've lost your direction."

Although it is seldom stated so succinctly, this is a lesson that Kerr teaches and reteaches throughout her books. People are not perfect, but those with "the right stuff" look up a lot more often than they look down.

Conclusion

At the Fifth International Conference on Humor held in Cork, Ireland, Lawrence Mintz, professor of American studies at the University of Maryland and coeditor of *Studies in American Humor,* analyzed the structure of typical situation comedies appearing on American television. He said that the premise of most sitcoms is that change is bad while the status quo is good.

Each show opens with a scene of normality, followed by the development of a problem. Actions taken by the characters, who attempt to solve the problem, only make it worse. But finally, when the situation appears totally hopeless, someone or something comes in from the outside to rescue the characters. Things return to normal and the show closes with a scene depicting the characters in a very similar position to the one they were in at the beginning.

In the situation comedy, the family is never really threatened. The problems are always the result of bad communication. The inherent, wish-fulfilling premise is that if people are honest and communicate with each other, then their problems will disappear and everything will be back to normal. Some sitcoms will titillate and tantalize viewers by mentioning a serious issue, but then the writers skirt that issue by making a joke. When people laugh, they are not so frightened. The overall effect and the reason for the appeal of the situation comedy is that it lulls viewers into a false sense of security.

Because Kerr says that her goal is to lure young people away from television and point them toward books instead, it is appropriate to compare what Kerr does in her books to what Lawrence Mintz says situation comedies do. Like the sitcoms, Kerr recommends honest communication to solve problems, and like the sitcoms she makes her readers laugh when a topic is uncomfortably serious. However, she does not bring up a serious issue only to skirt away from it with a joke. For example, her readers are well aware that Little Little's dwarfism is a real problem that is not going to go away no matter how honestly her family communicates or how cleverly Kerr makes jokes about it. In *Gentlehands,* no evidence—no surprise witnesses—come forth to prove that the story about Buddy's grandfather is a case of mistaken identity. In *If I Love You, Am I Trapped Forever?* Alan Bennett and Catherine Stein communicate wonderfully, but Mrs. Stein still runs away with the football coach. In *I Stay Near You,* even though Powell Storm and Mildred Cone are in love with each other, they do not get to marry and live happily ever after.

A second difference is that Kerr's protagonists do not circle around to end up at the same place they began. Early in the stories, they are preoccupied with themselves, but as the plots progress their views are enlarged and tempered by their experiences and interactions with other characters. Each book ends with the protagonist having arrived at a new level of maturity. For example, *What I Really Think of You* begins with Opal lamenting the hostility and the differences between herself and the "haves" who attend Seaville High. It ends with her expressing love for these same people: "When the Rapture comes, I want you all along, somehow, someway, every last one of you, ascending with me." *The Son of Someone Famous* begins with Brenda Belle terribly worried about her lack of acceptance and popularity and ends with her mother observing, "I have this feeling, this very definite feeling that you are slipping away from the crowd—that you are losing interest in the things other girls in Storm care about." *Gentlehands* begins with Buddy Boyle willing to do anything to look and act like a part of Skye's crowd. It ends with him consciously deciding to leave the navy blue cashmere sweater that Skye had given him in a heap on the floor of his grandfather's house among the tangled tapes of *Madame Butterfly* and *La traviata*. This symbolic gesture of leaving "everything about that summer behind me" illustrates a new acceptance of reality on Buddy's part.

The only one of Kerr's books that comes close to having the circular ending is *I'll Love You When You're More Like Me,* in which Wally Witherspoon resumes his courtship of Lauralei Rabinowitz. But even here Kerr is careful to point out one significant difference. Wally is no longer going to be an undertaker. He has managed to make that break with his father's expectations, an achievement not to be underestimated.

The third difference is that Kerr's characters solve their problems or adjust to them through their own actions. This may be as wish-fulfilling as the sitcoms, but at least the underlying premise is one of competence. Kerr's characters set an example of self-motivation. They take action instead of waiting passively to be rescued by the fates.

After reading an M. E. Kerr book and after watching a situation comedy, young adults may feel an equivalent sense of pleasure and security. But if Mintz's theory is correct, the feeling of security engendered by watching a situation comedy comes from the illusion that someone or something will always come along in time to save the protagonists from real danger. In contrast, readers of Kerr's books gain a feeling of security from identifying with the success of the characters, who use their own wits and strengths to solve their problems and/or adjust to those things that cannot be changed.

These three differences between situation comedies and Kerr's books are more than cosmetic. They are what make young readers active participants who vicariously become problem solvers rather than casual observers looking for a few hours of entertainment. And because of this, it is appropriate to borrow what E. B. White said at the end of *Charlotte's Web* when he paid tribute to the spider who saved Wilbur's life. Like Charlotte, M. E. Kerr is in a class by herself. Not often does someone come along who is a true teacher and a good writer. M. E. Kerr is both.

Appendix

Honors and Prizes Won by Kerr's Books

DINKY HOCKER SHOOTS SMACK!

Best of the Best Young Adult Books 1970–1983, American Library Association
Best Children's Books of 1972, *School Library Journal*
American Library Association Notable Children's Books of 1972
Media and Methods Maxi Award
Library of Congress Children's Books of 1972

GENTLEHANDS

Best Books for young Adults, 1978, American Library Association
American Library Association Notable Children's Books of 1978
Best Children's Books of 1978, *School Library Journal*
Winner, 1978 Christopher Award
Best Children's Books of 1978, *New York Times*

IF I LOVE YOU, AM I TRAPPED FOREVER?

Outstanding Children's Books of 1973, *New York Times*
Honor Book, *Book World* 1973 Children's Spring Book Festival

I'LL LOVE YOU WHEN YOU'RE MORE LIKE ME

Best Children's Books of 1977, *School Library Journal*
Outstanding Children's Books of 1977, *New York Times*

IS THAT YOU, MISS BLUE?

Outstanding Children's Books of 1975, *New York Times*
American Library Association Notable Children's Books of 1975
Best Books for Young Adults, 1975, American Library Association

LITTLE LITTLE

American Library Association Notable Children's Books of 1981
Best Books for Young Adults, 1981, American Library Association
Best Children's Books of 1981, *School Library Journal*
Winner, 1981 Golden Kite Award

ME ME ME ME ME: NOT A NOVEL

Best Books for Young Adults 1983, American Library Association

THE SON OF SOMEONE FAMOUS

Best Children's Books of 1974, *School Library Journal*
"Best of the Best" 1966–1978, *School Library Journal*

WHAT I REALLY THINK OF YOU

Best Children's Books of 1982, *School Library Journal*

Notes and References

1. Norma Fox Mazer, "I Love It! It's Your Best Book!" *English Journal,* February 1986, 26–29.

2. M. E. Kerr autobiography, *Something about the Author Autobiography Series* I:141–154, Detroit: Gale, 1986.

3. Mary Burns, *Horn Book*, August 1975, 385.

4. Mrs. John G. Gray, "Young People's Books," *Best Sellers* May 1975, 49.

5. Lillian Gerhardt, *School Library Journal,* November 1975, 176.

6. Ruth Charnes, *Interracial Books for Children Bulletin* 9, no. 8 (1978):18.

7. Kerr, autobiographical piece.

8. Marilyn Kaye, *New York Times Book Review,* 19 May 1981, 38.

9. *ALAN Review,* Fall 1983.

10. Nancy Hammond, *Horn Book,* December 1983, 462.

11. Stephen Dunning, "A Definition of the Role of the Junior Novel Based on Analyses of Thirty Selected Novels" (Ph.D. Diss., Florida State University, 1959).

12. M. E. Kerr, statement for "The People behind the Books," in *Literature for Today's Young Adults* by Alleen Pace Nilsen and Kenneth L. Donelson (Glenview, Ill.: Scott, Foresman, 1985).

13. Patricia Runk Sweeney, "Self-Discovery and Re-Discovery in the Novels of M. E. Kerr," *Lion and the Unicorn,* Fall 1978, 37–42.

14. Robert Unsworth, "Holden Caulfield, Where Are You?" *School Library Journal,* January 1977, 40–41.

15. Martin E. Marty, "We Need More Religion in Our Sitcoms," *TV Guide,* 24–30 December 1983, 2–6.

Selected Bibliography

Primary Sources

NOVELS

Dinky Hocker Shoots Smack! New York: Harper & Row, 1972; Dell, 1973.

Gentlehands. New York: Harper & Row, 1978; Bantam, 1979.

Him She Loves? New York: Harper & Row, 1984; Putnam, 1984.

I Stay Near You. New York: Harper & Row, 1985.

If I Love You, Am I Trapped Forever? New York: Harper & Row, 1973; Dell, 1974.

I'll Love You When You're More Like Me. New York: Harper & Row, 1977, Dell, 1979.

Is That You, Miss Blue? New York: Harper & Row, 1975; Dell, 1976.

Little Little. New York: Harper & Row, 1981; Scholastic, 1982.

Love Is a Missing Person. New York: Harper & Row, 1975; Dell, 1976.

ME ME ME ME ME: Not a Novel. New York: Harper & Row, 1983; New American Library, 1984.

The Son of Someone Famous. New York: Harper & Row, 1974; Ballantine, 1975.

What I Really Think of You. New York: Harper & Row, 1982; New American Library, 1983.

NONFICTION

Meaker, Marijane. *Sudden Endings.* New York: Doubleday, 1964; Vin Packer [pseud.]. Fawcett, n.d.

SHORT STORIES

Winston, Laura [pseud.]. *Compact* "The Character." (n.d.), 39–42, 88, 90, 92, 94.

————."Christmas Is a Funny Time of Year." *Compact* (n.d.), 34–36, 91–92, 94, 96–97.

————."Devotedly, Patrick Henry Casebolt." *Ladies' Home Journal* 68, no. 9 (September 1951):46–48, 226–28.

ARTICLES

Something about the Author Autobiography Series, I:141–154. Detroit: Gale, 1986.

"Feed the Wonder." *ALAN Review,* Fall 1982, 1–2.

Secondary Sources

BOOKS

Bryfonski, Dedria, ed. *Contemporary Literary Criticism,* 12:296–303. Detroit: Gale, 1980.

Commire, Anne, ed. *Something about the Author,* 20:124. Detroit: Gale, 1980.

Nilsen, Alleen P., and Kenneth L. Donelson. *Literature for Today's Young Adults.* Glenview, Ill.: Scott, Foresman, 1985.

ARTICLES

Delatiner, Barbara. "How 'Nancy Drew' Grew: Fiction for Young Adults." *New York Times,* 14 April 1974.

Janeczko, Paul. "An Interview with M. E. Kerr." *English Journal,* December 1975, 75–77.

Kingsbury, Mary. "The Why of People: The Novels of M. E. Kerr." *Horn Book,* June 1977, 288–95.

Mazer, Norma Fox. "I Love It! It's Your Best Book!" *English Journal,* February 1986, 26–29.

Piehl, Kathy. "The Business of Religion in M. E. Kerr's Novels." *VOYA,* February 1985, 307–10, 363.

Scholastic *Voice.* "Spotlight on M. E. Kerr and *Little Little.*" Interview reprinted in Scholastic Catalogue, 1982.

Sweeney, Patricia Runk. "Self-Discovery and Re-Discovery in the Novels of M. E. Kerr." *Lion and the Unicorn,* Fall 1978, 37–42.

Tallmer, Jerry. "An Old Question for Young Adults." *New York Post,* 8 July 1978.

Unsworth, Robert. "Holden Caulfield, Where are You?" *School Library Journal.* January 1977, 40–41.

SELECTED BOOK REVIEWS

DINKY HOCKER SHOOTS SMACK!

Buckley, Tom. "TV: Afterschool Gluttony." *New York Times,* 15 November 1978, C-30.
Elementary English, October 1973, 1098.
Horn Book, February 1973, 56.
Kirkus Reviews, 1 October 1972, 1152–53.
New York Times Book Review, 11 February 1973, 8.
Pollack, Pamela D. *School Library Journal,* December 1972, 73.
Rosenberg, Howard. "Dinky Hocker on ABC." *Los Angeles Times,* 15 November 1978, IV:28.

GENTLEHANDS

Bradford, Richard. "The Nazi Legacy: Undoing History." *New York Times Book Review,* 30 April 1978, 30.
Denver Post, 28 May 1978, 20.
Horn Book, June 1978, 284–85.
Sutherland, Zena. *Chicago Tribune Book Review,* 2 July 1978.
Tallmer, Jerry. "Grandpa was Special." *New York Post,* 8 July 1978.

HIM SHE LOVES?

Horn Book, June 1984, 339.
Webb, Kay. *School Library Journal,* August 1984, 84.

I STAY NEAR YOU

Bulletin of the Center for Children's Books, June 1985, 188.
Tyson, Christy, *VOYA,* June 1985, 132.

IF I LOVE YOU, AM I TRAPPED FOREVER?

Elementary English, September 1973, 945–46.
Gersoni-Stavn, Diane. *School Library Journal,* April 1973, 75.
Horn Book, June 1973, 276–77.
New York Times Book Review, 16 September 1973, 8.
School Library Journal, April 1973, 75.

I'LL LOVE YOU WHEN YOU'RE MORE LIKE ME

Hill, Evelyn. *News from ALAN,* Spring 1978.
Horn Book, December 1977, 668–69.
Interracial Books for Children Bulletin, no. 3 (1978): 14.
New York Times Book Review, 13 November 1977, 50.
Nilsen, Alleen Pace. *English Journal,* February 1978, 99.

IS THAT YOU, MISS BLUE?

Best Sellers, May 1975, 49.
Burns, Mary M. *Horn Book,* August 1975, 365.
Lion and the Unicorn, Fall 1978, 37–42.

LITTLE LITTLE

Abrahamson, Dick. *English Journal,* September 1981, 77.
Horn Book, June 1981, 309–10.
Karlin, Barbara. *Los Angeles Times Book Review,* 23 August 1981, 7.
Kaye, Marilyn. *New York Times Book Review,* 19 May 1981, 38.

LOVE IS A MISSING PERSON

Bulletin of the Center for Children's Books, November 1975, 48.
Gerhardt, Lillian N. *School Library Journal,* November 1975, 176.
Publishers Weekly, 30 June 1975, 58.

ME ME ME ME ME

Horn Book, December 1983, 462.
Lewis, Marjorie. *School Library Journal,* August 1983, 77–78.
Milton, Joyce. *New York Times Book Review,* 22 May 1983, 39.
Reed, Arthea J. S. *ALAN Review,* Fall 1983.

THE SON OF SOMEONE FAMOUS

Horn Book, August 1974, 384–85.
New York Times Book Review, 7 April 1974, 8.
New Yorker, 2 December 1974, 187–88.

WHAT I REALLY THINK OF YOU

Kaye, Marilyn. *New York Times Book Review.* 12 September 1982, 49–50.
Shapiro, Lillian L. *School Library Journal.* May 1982, 71–72.

Index

About the Author

Alleen Pace Nilsen is professor of education and assistant dean of the graduate college at Arizona State University where she teaches literature for young readers. With Ken Donelson, she is coeditor of the *English Journal* and coauthor of *Literature for Today's Young Adults*. Also with Donelson, she was the founding editor of the *ALAN Review* published by the Assembly on Literature for Adolescents, National Council of Teachers of English. In 1978–79, she was president of this organization which is devoted to the promotion and improvement of literature for teenagers. Nilsen's articles on young adult literature have appeared in *Top of the News, English Journal, School Library Journal, Iowa English Bulletin, Language Arts, the ALAN Review, Journal of Reading,* and *Arizona English Bulletin.*